TOMBSTONE CLIPPINGS

Edited by

Ben T. Traywick

Ben T. Traywick

Published by:

Red Marie's Bookstore
P.O. Box 891
Tombstone, Arizona 85638

Designed and Printed by:
WE PRINT IT, INC.
—Los Angeles—

To the Tombstone

Newspaper Reporters

of the 1880's.

Published by
Red Marie's Bookstore

Designed and Printed by
WE PRINT IT, INC,
—Los Angeles—

Subject Guide v

TABLE OF CONTENTS

Photographs

NEWS PUBLISHERS OF TOMBSTONE AND SOUTHEAST ARIZONA

NEWSPAPER BANNERS

NEWSPAPER EDITORIALS

PHOTOGRAPHERS OF TOMBSTONE

NEWS ARTICLES

SUBJECT GUIDE

PUBLISHED NOTICES

SOME FAMOUS NAMES IN TOMBSTONE HISTORY

GOVERNMENT AGENTS, OFFICERS ELECTED OFFICIALS & APPOINTEES

MILITARY OFFICERS

MEXICAN OFFICIALS

MINISTERS IN THE NEWS

ORGANIZATIONS LOCATED IN TOMBSTONE

DOCTORS AND DENTISTS OF TOMBSTONE

BANKS LOCATED ABOUT TOMBSTONE

ATTORNIES OF TOMBSTONE

THEATRES OF TOMBSTONE AND FEATURED ARTISTS

ACTORS APPEARING IN TOMBSTONE

ACTRESSES APPEARING IN TOMBSTONE

CIRCUS SHOWS VISITING TOMBSTONE

RED LIGHT (HELL'S BELLES) ESTABLISHMENT IN PRINT

HOTELS LOCATED ABOUT TOMBSTONE AND VICINITY

RESTAURANTS LOCATED ABOUT TOMBSTONE

SALOONS OF TOMBSTONE AND ARIZONA TERRITORY

UNDERTAKERS OF TOMBSTONE

OTHER BUSINESSES LOCATED ABOUT TOMBSTONE & VICINITY

PROPRIETORS OF BUSINESSES LOCATED ABOUT TOMBSTONE

AGENTS OF BUSINESSES LOCATED ABOUT TOMBSTONE

SUPERVISORS OF BUSINESSES LOCATED ABOUT TOMBSTONE

MANAGERS OF BUSINESSES LOCATED ABOUT TOMBSTONE

CITIZENS OF TOMBSTONE IN PRINT

CITIZENS OF CHARLESTON, A.T., IN PRINT

CITIZENS OF GLEESON, A.T., IN PRINT

CITIZENS OF WILLCOX, A.T., IN PRINT

CITIZENS OF WILLIAMS, A.T. IN PRINT

STAGE PASSENGERS IN THE NEWS

LANDMARKS AND LOCATIONS

POEM ABOUT THE FAMOUS...

The Tombstone Epitaph office, 1880.
At that time, the Epitaph office had a balcony.

EDITOR'S FOREWORD

Tombstone had a variety of newspapers. Some were not in business long and others underwent mergers and sell-outs.

They were:

Tombstone Epitaph
Tombstone Nugget
Tombstone American Republican
Tombstone Daily Epitaph and Republican
Tombstone Daily Democrat
Tombstone Prospector
Cochise Daily Record
Daily Record – Epitaph
Daily Tombstone
Arizona Kicker
Evening Gossip
Independent
The American
Valley Herald
Borderland Times

The newspaper items the reader will find in this volume were taken from the yellowed files of the town's old newspapers.

EDITOR'S FOREWORD (continued)

They are untouched and unchanged–just as they were printed over a hundred years ago. Here, one will read exactly what a citizen would have read in Tombstone during the mining days. These clippings and advertisements relate the history that was Tombstone, establishing locations, dates and identifying business owners as well as recounting events that happened during the turbulent times.

This is a book that could well be counted valuable and should be found in the reference library of every historian and writer.

We hope you enjoy this journey into the past as you read through these pages taken directly from history.

Ben T. Traywick
Editor

WEEKLY EPITAPH.

TOMBSTONE, ARIZONA, - - MAY 1, 1880.

TERMS, INCLUDING POSTAGE:

One Year	$5 00
Six Months	3 00
Three Months	1 75
Monthly, delivered by carrier	50

For sale by all news dealers.

CLUM, SORIN & CO., Proprietors.

THE FIRST TRUMPET.

Tombstone is a city set upon a hill, promising to vie with ancient Rome, upon her seven hills, in a fame different in character but no less in importance. Scarcely a year has passed since the limits of the townsite were proclaimed and the hardy pioneer settler raised the first structure of human abode. To-day Tombstone affords over 500 roofs for the shelter of man and beast, with a population of about four to each of the aforesaid sheltering roofs. To this sturdy, prosperous population and the public in general—on this bright, bran new May morning, our natal day, the first May morning in the new decade of 1880—the Epitaph tends a hearty and cordial greeting. No tombstone is complete without its epitaph and so we have come to fill the void and make all happy in the consequent perfection.

The Epitaph is issued to-day because the courage and perseverance of the prospector and the honest, constant toil of the miner has opened a great field of usefulness for it and made it not only possible but highly desirable that a journal of its character should be created here in order that the mineral wonders in this district might be brought fully and properly before the great public. The Epitaph accepts this important duty as its own and shall use every endeavor to fulfill its obligations with credit to itself and satisfaction to its patrons. Since the prospector and miner have paved the way to our existence we recognize it as our duty and pleasure, in reciprocation, to bend every influence and energy for the advancement of their interests.

The policy of the paper may be summed up in the words, honesty and accuracy. Its columns are at the disposal of all who have reliable reports from good properties, and wild cats are requested to pass by on the other side, as we shall take no pet kittens to raise.

A special feature of the Epitaph, which we hope will be at once instructive and popular, will be the most accurate representation possible of all the prominent mines of this district, including exhaustive descriptive and statistical matter, accompanied by surface and sectional diagrams of the works and developments on the respective mines. These diagrams will be copied from plats carefully prepared by skillful engineers and our descriptive matter will be compiled from official statistics and personal obervation. These reports can be relied upon and a complete file of the Epitaph will constitute a comprehensive record of the development of the Tombstone mines. We trust our patrons will profit by this hint.

The Epitaph is Republican in sympathy, but will be devoted rather to local interests than to national politics. It is our purpose to build up a representative mining journal—one that can be relied upon at home and abroad. Our observations will include Territorial and general mining notes, but more particularly Pima County interests and especially the resources and developments of Tombstone District. And in the discharge of these great and arduous duties we hope for the co-operation and support of all who desire progress and prosperity in this direction. We intend to make a paper that will be much sought after, both as a medium of advertising and news one that shall at once command a power and influence in the land; and hoping to direct this power in proper channels for the attainment of just aims we will lay aside our "gray goose quill" and say to all: Halloo!

May 1, 1880

GENERAL MERCHANDISE.

May 1, 1880

W. A. EASTMAN,

CARPENTER AND BUILDER

Orders Promptly Attended to.

Shop on Fremont Street—EPITAPH BLOCK.

TOMBSTONE STORE,

R. R. GOODE, PROPRIETOR,

DEALER IN

General Merchandise.

COMPLETE OUTFIT FOR PROSPECTORS.

California Made Boots and Clothing.

The Best Assorted Stock of Family Groceries in Tombstone District.

MARK P. SHAFFER,

Business Manager.

EATON & RICE,

—Dealers in—

DRUGS AND MEDICINES

Toilet Articles. Patent Medicine.

Physicians prescriptions carefully compounded day and night. Store on Allen Street.

Go to

CADWELL & STANFORD'S

To Fill Your Orders.

GENERAL MERCHANDISE; MINers' Supplies a Specialty.

U. S. MARKET,

A. BAUER, - - - Proprietor.

Fresh Beef, Mutton, Veal, Pork, Corned Beef and Sausage,

Constantly on hand.

ONLY AMERICAN BEEF KILLED.

WILL FURNISH QUARTERS OR SIDES of beef at seven cents per pound, for cash. Mutton at the same price, per carcass.

Retail Prices Reduced to the Lowest Figure.

☞ Meat Delivered in Camp Free of Charge. ☜

POMEROY & GREER,

Dealers in

DRUGS, MEDICINES, WINES

TOILET AND FANCY ARTICLES, PERfumeries, Etc., ALLEN STREET, near corner of Fourth.

TOMBSTONE, ARIZONA.

WATCHMAKERS AND JEWELERS.

J. M. BERGER,

WATCHMAKER & JEWELER

Opposite Pima County Bank, Tucson.

DEALER IN WATCHES AND CLOCKS, Diamonds, Jewelry, Sewing Machines, Sewing Machine Attachments, Needles and Oil. Watch repairing a specialty. Agent for Sherman, Hyde & Co. Pianos, Organs and Brass Instruments.

PAUL PLUMMER,

DEALER IN

WATCHES, CLOCKS, JEWELRY, Spectacles and Eye-Glasses, all kinds Musical Instruments, Violin Strings, Stationery, Cutlery, Sewing Machines, Needles, etc., **Church Plaza, near Congress street, Tucson, Arizona.**

PHOTOGRAPHERS.

H. BUEHMAN,

PHOTOGRAPHER,

Maiden Lane and Congress Streets, Tucson, Arizona.

With New and Enlarged Facilities is prepared to do all kinds of work in the highest style of the art. Keeps also on hand a complete assortment of **Arizona Views**, Picture Frames, Moulding, Chromos, Etc.

May 1, 1880

GUNSMITH.

G. F. Spangenberg,

PRACTICAL

GUNSMITH and MACHINIST,

In Tin Shop, Fourth st., near Post Office.

REPAIRER OF GUNS, PISTOLS, LOCKS and all kinds of sewing machines, key-fitting, sewing machine needles, oil and attachments.

N. B.—All work warranted.

Harness Shop,

Opposite Mark Shaffer's, Fremont St., Tombstone.

WHERE CAN BE FOUND A GOOD ASsortment of **HARNESS, COLLARS, BRIDLES, LINES, HALTERS, PACK SADDLES, etc.** In fact everything in our line all first class and at bed rock prices.

Prospectors fitted out on short notice. Repairing done promptly and at reasonable rates.

D. R. M. THOMPSON, Pro.

THE NEVADA

BOOT AND SHOE STORE,

ALLEN ST., NEAR FIFTH,

MISS NELLIE CASHMAN, PROprietress. Gentlemen's furnishing goods a specialty.

A Large Assortment of Ladies' and Children's Shoes on hand. Customers and orders will receive prompt attention from

MISS KATE O'HARA, Managing.

Proposals for Ore Hauling.

PROPOSALS WILL BE RECEIVED AT THE office of the Tombstone Mill and Mining Company, Millville, A. T., until 12 o'clock m. on the 15th day of May, 1880, for hauling ore from the mines of the company in Tombstone District to the Gird Mill, at Millville, A. T., for the term of one year, commencing June 1, 1880.

The Superinnendent reserves the right to reject any or all bids, as the good of the company may require.

RICHARD GIRD,
Superintendent.

GENERAL MERCHANDISE.

M. EDWARDS,

CALIFORNIA VARIETY STORE!

Corner Allen and Fourth Streets. TOMBSTONE.

Wholesale and Retail Dealer in General Merchandise.

KEEPS CONSTANTLY ON HAND A LARGE stock of all kinds of goods and sells

CHEAP FOR CASH.

COME AND SEE FOR YOURSELF.

J. M. CASTANEDA, - - MANAGER.

CITY BAKERY,

ALLEN STREET.

FRESH BREAD AND ROLLS EVERY DAY.

Rye and Graham Bread.

☞ PIES, CAKES AND CANDIES ALWAYS ON HAND

O. M. GEISENHOFER.

May 1, 1880

Tombstone & Tucson

STAGE LINE,

LEAVING RAILROAD TERMINUS EVERY day at 8 a. m. Concord Coaches are run on this line. Good meals en route at reasonable rates. Fare, $7, Currency.

All orders should be left at the Stage and Express Office, in Eaton & Rice's Drug Store, Tombstone, where they will receive prompt attention.

Passengers will register and pay fare at the office

J. D. KINNEAR, Prop.

JOE EATON, Office Agent, Tombstone.

HOTELS AND RESTAURANTS.

Headquarters Kinnear's Stage Company.

Cosmopolitan Hotel !!

THE LARGEST HOTEL IN THE DISTRICT. Having completed my second story addition, I am enabled to offer the traveling public very superior accommodations.

Table Supplied with Everything the Market Affords.

Thankful to my friends for past patronage, I respectfully solicit a continuance of the same.

C. BILICKE, PROPRIETOR.

May 1, 1880

TRANSPORTATION.

NEW

Tombstone AND Terminus

Daily Stage Line,

CARRYING

United States Mail and Wells Fargo Express.

H. C. WALKER & CO., PROP.

FASTEST TIME, BEST ROADS, LOWEST Rates. Leave Tucson and Tombstone Daily at 7 a. m.

MARSHALL WILLIAMS,
Agent, Tombstone.

J. C. NICHOLS, Agent, Tucson.
C. A. BARTHOLOMEW, Superintendent.

May 1, 1880

LUMBER, BUILDERS' MATERIAL, CROCKERY, ETC.

ROBERT ECCLESTON,
FREEMONT STREET, TOMBSTONE.

A. D. OTIS,
MAIN STREET, TUCSON.

A. D. OTIS & CO.,

DEALERS IN

Lumber and Shingles, Doors, Windows, and Blinds,

Builders' and General Hardware, Paints, Oils, Glass, Etc. Crockery, Glassware, Lamps and Chandeliers; Carpenters', Builders' and Painters' Supplies.

P. W. SMITH,

General Merchandise and Banker,

Cor. Allen and Fourth Streets, Tombstone.

SUNNYSIDE HOTEL.

MRS. M. YOHO, Prop.

Nice, quiet, clean and desirable rooms for the traveling public. Centrally located. One block from the depot.

Rooms by the Day, Week or Month at Reasonable Rates.

Fourth Street Bet. Allen & Toughnut. - - - Tombstone, Arizona.

Arcade Hotel...

Opposite Depot.

Newly Furnished and Renovated

Throughout, under new management. Rooms large and airy. An inviting place for the traveler to stop during a stay. in Tombstone.

MRS. GEO. BLACK. Propritress.

Tombstone Corral,

Fremont St., bet. Second an Thir

(Opposite Sam Light's old place.)

H. H. TUTTLE

Has again taken charge of this well-known Corral, and is preparing

Accommodations for 100 Horses,

And wishes to inform his patrons and the public generally that he will conduct the business on the same popular plan as when he formerly had charge of the same.

GOOD SADDLE HORSES FOR HIRE,
And prices reasonable. Plenty of room, and stock carefully attended to.

A competent man will be found at my stables at all times to attend to the wants of customers.

☞ DON'T FORGET THE PLACE.

Fremont St. bet. Second and Third.

G. B. WATT. C. B. TARBELL.

Watt & Tarbell,

UNDERTAKERS

No. 418 Allen Street.

(Next door to Hare & Page's Livery Stable.)

UNDERTAKING AND EMBALMING

In all its Branches. Preparing and Removing bodies promptly attended also.

Orders filled on short notice from any part of the County. Night orders can be left at Hare & Page's Livery Stable.

Tombstone Carriage

SHOP,

GEORGE L. OTT, Third Street.

WE ARE PREPARED TO DO ALL KINDS of Carriage and Wagon work on short notice, and will Guarantee satisfaction and Reasonable Prices. We also give particular attention to Horseshoeing and Miners' Work.

From long experience in the business and the many testimonials received from our customers we feel warranted in saying that we can give satisfaction.

GIVE US A TRIAL.

FASHION SALOON

Just Opened.

Opposite the Cosmopolitan Hotel,

—ON—

ALLEN STREET,

—AND—

KEPT BY D. T. MOONEY.

HIS ENTIRE STOCK IS WARRANTED TO be of the best ever dispensed in the territory. All are invited to test it.

The Alhambra.

T. H. CORRIGAN, - - Proprietor.

Elegantly re-fitted and just re-opened with the finest stock of Wines, Liquors and Cigars ever brought to Tombstone.

My stock embraces the famous O. K., Cutter, Hermitage, Old Government and Stonewall brands. Imported Brandies. My wines and liquors have been especially selected for the Tombstone trade and can not be surpassed for age and bouquet. Cigars were made to order and of the choicest Havana tobaccos.

The Old Boys are notified that the Latch String is always on the outside

Arizona Mail and Stage Line.

J. D. KINNEAR & CO., Proprietors

Lowest Stage Rates.

TOMBSTONE TO BENSON DAILY!
TOMBSTONE TO CHARLESTON DAILY!
TOMBSTONE TO HUACHUCA TRI-WEEKLY!
TOMBSTONE TO HARSHAW TRI-WEELLY!
TOMBSTONE TO CONTENTION CITY DAILY!
TOMBSTONE TO BISBEE TRI-WEEKLY.

Coaches can be Chartered from Benson to Tombstone and Return by Giving Two Days Notice.

Fastest Time and Best Stock.

OFFICE WITH WELLS, FARGO & CO., TOMBSTONE.

MARSHALL WILLIAMS, AGENT.

RUSS HOUSE,

CORNER OF FIFTH AND TOUGH NUT STREETS.

Tombstone, Arizona.

UNDER A NEW MANAGEMENT.

Miss NELLIE CASHMAN and MR. JOSEPH PASCHOLY HAVING taken charge of this new and popular house, beg to announce to to their friends and the traveling public that it is their determination to run it first class in every particular. Having already a reputation of knowing "how to keep a hotel," it shall be their endeavor to maintain that reputation. Cal and be convinced.

THE BEST DRESSED MAN IN TOWN!

—WEARS A SUIT OF—

Clothes Cut and Made

—BY—

SAM'L BLACK,

THE TAILOR,

206 FOURTH STREET,

NEAR BROWN'S HOTEL,

Tombstone, A. T

WHERE YOU WILL FIND THE BEST SELECTED STOCK OF IMPORTED WOOLEN Cassimeres, Diagonals, Broadcloths, Scotch and English Cheviots, Fancy Suitings and Trousering, and the Latest Fashions at Bed-Rock Prices. A perfect fit and first-class workmanship guaranteed. Scouring and Steaming by the latest process, and Binding and Repairing at Reduced Rates. Call and examine the Goods and Prices before going elsewhere.

206 Fourth Street, near Brown's Hotel.

G. F. SPANGENBERG,

PIONEER GUNSMITH

Locksmith. AND

212 FOURTH STREET. NEAR BROWN'S HOTEL.

DEALER IN GUNS, PISTOLS, CARTRIDGES, CUTLERY, SEWING MACHINES, Etc.

The Only Complete Gun and Locksmithing Shop in Arizona

July 23, 1882

MISCELLANEOUS.

LIVERY & FEED STABLE!
CARRIAGES & BUGGIES
Single and Double.

Saddle Horses can always be procured at reasonable rates. Special care taken of Transient Stock.

J. O. DUNBAR,
ALLEN STREET, Bet. THIRD & FOURTH
next to P. W. Smith's

BATHS!

Hot and Cold Baths!

FREMONT STREET,
Next Door to Baron's Barber Shop.
je20 tf

For CONTENTION

SANDY BOB'S LINE

Stages to connect with the Eastbound Train leave at 5 a. m.

Stages to connect with the Westbound train leave at 1:00 p. m.

Accommodation stage leaves every day for Contention at 2:30 p. m.

Office—At Wells. Fargo & Co's Express Office.

NOTICE.

All Parties who are Indebted
TO THE
AMERICAN CLOTHING CO.,
ARE HEREBY
Notified to Call and Settle
As there has been
A CHANGE IN THE FIRM,
And all outstanding accounts must be Settled at Once.

American Clothing
COMPANY.
jy13 2w

November 11, 1880
(Ackerson found dead)

Jerry Ackerson Found Dead at Croton Springs With a Bullet Through His Brain—No Clue to the Murderers.

On Sunday evening our town was startled by the report that Jerry Ackerso a well known citizen, had been found dead near Croton Springs, on the line of the Southern Pacific, about thirty-five miles from Tombstone. The report was not at first generally credited, but inquiry of Deputy Sheriff Earp confirmed the sad tidings It came in the nature of a dispatch from Bob Paul, stating that Ackerson had been murdered, and asking in whose company he had left Tombstone. Diligent inquiry on the part of the officers failed to elicit any information on this point, further than that Ackerson had left town on Friday night some time, and it was thought unattended. Rumors as to the cause of the murder were rife. It was suggested that Ackerson, prior to leaving town, had sold his interests in mines and property, amounting to a considerable sum, and had taken some four or five thousand dollars with him, intending to purchase cattle from some of the San Simon party who were here a few days ago. This rumor proved to be without foundation, as about $100, it seems, was all the money he had in his possession when he left That he was murdered for this paltry sum seems hardly probable. When found he was lying face down on the ground, with his Winchester rifle tightly grasped in his hands, the left arm extended as if in the act of firing. One cartridge was gone from the chamber, and the barrel of the weapon was grimed with smoke. He was shot just below the left ear, the ball passing through and coming out of the right temple. His funeral took place at Wilcox yesterday morning. The following short biography is all that we have been able to glean: Jerome B. Ackerson was born in the State of New York, and at the time of his death was about 38 years of age. He has been on the Pacific Coast about 10 years, residing most of that time in Southern California. He was among the pioneers of Tombstone, and was regarded as one of its best citizens. Brave as a lion and generous to a fault, his tragic and untimely death is sincerely mourned by a host of friends to whom he had endeared himself by the amenities of life. To his bereaved family in Iowa the EPITAPH, in common with the whole community, tenders sympathy in their great bereavement.

THE DAILY NUGGET

The Official Paper of the Village.

TOMBSTONE, NOVEMBER [illegible], 1880.

WATERMAN & GOODRICH,

—DEALERS IN—

Hardware, Stoves, Tinware,

SHEET IRON, COPPER, &c.

Sixth Street, between Allen and Fremont Sts.,

Tombstone, Arizona.

Manufacturing and Repairing done neatly and promptly.

The Arizona Corral,

Cor. Allen & Third Streets,

GARRISON & SPANGLER,

PROPRIETORS.

Boarding & Feed Stable.

Elegant Turnouts and the Best Stock in the City. Saddle Horses not to be Excelled. Boarding and Transient taken Cheaper than any other Corral in Tombstone.

CALL AND SEE FOR YOURSELVES.

Cal. Fruit Depot,

C. J. EASTMAN & CO.,

Opposite Grand Hotel, Tombstone

All Fruit for this house is picked fresh from the vines and trees and packed by a member of the firm in Los Angeles.

Neff always at home in the store and glad to see his friends.

1on

Lord & Williams,

Dealers in

GENERAL

Merchandise,

TUCSON, ARIZONA.

MILL & MINING SUPPLIES

A Specialty.

A Large Stock of

LUMBER ALWAYS ON HAND

And contracts for furnishing same delivered at destination, taken at bottom prices.

Sole Agents in Southern Arizona for the celebrated

ANHEUSER BEER

The Finest Brands of

LIQUORS AND CIGARS

Always on hand, at prices to suit purchasers.

For Village Marshal.

I hereby announce myself as a candidate for Village Marshal at the election on the 12th day of November. V. W. EARP

For Village Marshal.

I hereby announce myself as a candidate for Village Marshal at the election on the 12th day of November. BENJ. SIPPY.

For City Marshal.

I hereby announce myself as a candidate for the office of City Marshal, subject to the suffrages of the people of Tombstone. JAS. FLYNN.

Tombstone, November 2, 1880.

DAILY EPITAPH.

PIONEER DAILY OF THE CAMP.

THURSDAY MORNING, - - AUGUST 26, 1880

PUBLISHED EVERY MORNING,
(Mondays Excepted)
—BY—
CLUM, SORIN & CO.

T. R. SORIN.............................Editor.
J. P. CLUM....................Business Manager.

Office on FREMONT STREET, North Side, between Third and Fourth.

SUBSCRIPTION RATES:

Daily Epitaph, delivered, per week.............$ 25c
Daily and Weekly, del'd, per week........... .. 35c
☞ Weekly Epitaph, delivered every Saturday evening for 50c a month. By mail: One year, $5; Six months, $3; Three months, $1.50.

Successful Amputation.

On the 2d of July last, Frank Bowles, formerly of New Valde, Texas, accidentally shot himself in the leg near the knee. At the time of the shooting Bowles was near Fort Bowie, and went there for surgical relief, which he says was refused him. Suffice it that he remained there forty-one days without medical attendance, his leg gradually growing worse, when Billy Hutchins, hearing of the misfortune of his old friend, had him brought to Tombstone, employed medical skill, and he and his good wife have nursed and tended him assiduously since. From the first his attending physician despaired of saving the leg, and yesterday a consultation of physicians was held, and the amputation of the leg above the knee resolved upon. The patient was placed under the influence of anæsthetics, and the operation skillfully performed by Dr. Giberson, assisted by Drs. Matthews and Creer. The patient, though an eld[illegible] man, stood [illegible] operation well, rallying nicely after it, and the physicians have strong hopes of his ultimate recovery.

The Parlor Bathing and Shaving Saloon

Is the name of a new ornament to the corner of Allen and Fourth streets, which is this morning opened to the public through the enterprise and business foresight of Mr. W. Barron, who has recently come among us from the city of the Golden Gate. Neither skill nor expense have been spared by Mr. Barron in giving to the people of Tombstone a bathing and shaving saloon complete in all its appointments, and when completed there will not be another on this side of San Francisco of finer finish. The chairs are of the latest improved style, shipped direct from the Rochester factory, the mirrors will be of the finest French plate and the bath rooms are supplied with all the necessaries for the enjoyment of a shower, hot or cold water bath. We bespeak for Mr. Barron that patronage which his energy and liberality deserve. Give him a call.

August 26, 1880

. ARIZONA. THURSDAY MORNING. AUGUST 26. 1880

TOMBSTONE FOUNDRY.

TOMBSTONE  FOUNDRY

And Machine Shop!

Corner First and Safford Streets.

T. S. HARRIS.......................................PROPRIETOR

☞Iron and Brass Castings of all kinds made to order. Machine Work, Wood Turning and Blacksmithing. MILL WORK A SPECIALTY. Cash paid for Old Iron and Brass.

PLUMBING AND STEAM-FITTING.

T. A. Atchison,

Pioneer Plumber and Steam Fitter,

FOURTH STREET, TOMBSTONE,
Three Doors Above POST OFFICE.

☞Having conducted this line of business for years in the States, and possessing a Complete Outfit of Machinery and Tools, I am prepared to do all work in this line in the best manner possible.

ROOFING A SPECIALTY.

Orders Filled Promptly and LOW for Cash. Stoves, Granite Ware, Tinware, Wire, Etc., and all Miners' Outfits constantly on hand.

TRANSPORTATION.

Accommodation DAIY Line to BENSON!

CROUCH & CO., Proprietors.

$2.00 LEAVE TOMBSTONE DAILY AT 5 P. M. $2.00

FARE, $2, Office at Harry Hubbard's Ice House, Fifth Street.

Opposition Line to Benson!

☞INGRAHAM & CO. are now running a DAILY STAGE LINE to BENSON,

Leaving Tombstone Daily at 5 P. M. Fare, $3.

G. W. CHAPMAN, AGENT,

Office in Doling's Block, Opposite the Cosmopolitan Hotel.

LIQUOR DEALERS—WHOLESALE AND RETAIL.

KELLY'S WINE ROOMS,

J. A. KELLY, PROPRIETOR.

Fremont Street, Near Fourth, and Allen Street, Near Fifth.

TOMBSTONE, ARIZONA.

Keeps Constantly on hand a Large Stock of the CHOICEST BRANDS of WINES, LIQUORS and CIGARS, both Imported and Domestic. We retail at the Sideboard nothing but

O. K. Cutter and Miller's Extra Whiskies,

And the Very Choicest Brands of WINES, LIQUORS and CIGARS.

GENUINE ENGLISH ALE AND MAHLSTEDT'S CELEBRATED LOS ANGELES LAGER BEER ON DRAUGHT, and a Large Stock of Genuine BLOOD'S PORTER and TENNENT'S ALE in bottles and cases.

☞ We always have an abundance of ICE when it is to be had. ALL DRINKS 12 1-2 CENTS.

PRICE LIST PER BOTTLE.

O K Cutter Whisky	$1 50
Miller's Extra	1 50
Fine Old California Brandy	1 50
Fine Old Kentucky Apple Brandy (6 years old)	1 75
Sweet Wine (5 years old) from Muscat Grapes	75
Fine Old Angelica Wine (5 years old	75
Fine Old Port Wine (5 years old).	75
Fine Imported Sherry	1 25
Genuine Imported French Claret	1 00
" " " "	1 25
Choice California Claret	50
Choice California White Wine	50

And many other Wines and Liquors at equally low prices. **Special inducements offered to the trade** in all goods in our line.

GUNSMITHING.

HART'S GUN SHOP,

SIGN OF THE BIG REVOLVER AND KEY, FREMONT ST.,

Is the place to get all kinds of GUN WORK done in a workmanlike manner and warranted. Locks repaired and keys fitted, Engraving, Wood and Iron turning, and repairs on anything done on short notice. S. L. HART.

G. F. SPANGENBERG.

PIONEER

Gun and Locksmiths,

FOURTH STREET, NEAR POST OFFICE.

DEALERS IN GUNS, PISTOLS, CARTRIDGES, CUTLERY, SEWING MACHINES, Etc.

The Only Complete Gun and Locksmithing Shop in Arizona

The Branch White House,

COSMOPOLITAN HOTEL BUILDING, TOMBSTONE.

Just received, a large and well selected stock of

Millinery, Fancy Dry Goods, Ladies' Suits, Wrappers, Ulsters and a Complete Assortment of Underwear.

ALSO, A FINE LINE OF GENTS' UNDERWEAR.

Goods sold CHEAP and for CASH ONLY.

THEO WELISCH & CO.

Golden Eagle Brewery

Finest Liquors 12 1-2 CENTS.

Choicest Cigars, 12 1-2 CENTS.

BEER:

Ten Gallons $6.00

Five 3.00

Bottles, per dozen three dollars.

3 Bottles for $1.00 in Saloon

WEHRFRITZ & TRIBOLET, Proprietors.

ALLEN STREET, Cor. of Fifth, TOMBSTONE.

Beer Delivered in any part of the Village.

MAND'S WINE HOUSE,

OPENED MAY 8, 1880.

O.K. Cutter, Millers Extra Whiskies. RETAILED AT THE SIDEBOARD.

Drinks 12 1-2 Cents.

Wines, Liquors and Cigars--Choicest Brands, BOTH IMPORTED AND DOMESTIC.

Special Inducements Offered to the Trade, and to the Public, when Wines, Liquors and Cigars are sold in quantity.

☞ A Cosy READING ROOM, with all the latest Newspapers, Pictorials and Magazines. Also, NEAT CLUB ROOMS, where gentlemen can congregate together without being disturbed by outsiders.

GIVE US A CALL.

FREMONT STREET, NEAR FOURTH, TOMBSTONE, ARIZONA.

July 22, 1880

TOMBSTONE, ARIZONA, THURSDAY MORNING, JULY 22.

I. X. L. LACE HOUSE.

THE ONE-PRICE

I X L Lace Store,

L. COHEN, Proprietor.

Fremont Street, Opposite Post Office.

Laces, Edgings, Embroideries, Pillow Case Lace.

LADIES',
MISSES' and
CHILDREN'S

Hosiery!

Mr. L. Cohen takes pleasure in announcing to the Tombstone public that he has opened a CHOICE LINE of Embroideries, Laces, Edgings, Etc., Etc., on Fremont Street, opposite the Post Office, at the Millinery Store, formerly conducted by Mrs. S. E. Fallon.

Having purchased the Entire Line of Millinery, it will be Closed Out, REGARDLESS of COST.

LADIES, take notice that you can buy at the New I X L Store
Spool Cotton for 5c;
Lace Edging at 5c a yard;
EmbroiderieS from 12 1-2c upward
Ladies', Misses' and Children's Hosiery, Striped in all Colors, at 25c per pair.

All Goods will be sold in proportion, at San Francisco Prices.

CHEAP FOR CASH
AND CASH ONLY.

AMERICAN ONE-PRICE STORE.

THE AMERICAN

One-Price

STORE,

MIDDLE STORE,

VIZINA & COOK BLOCK, BETWEEN FIFTH AND SIXTH, ON ALLEN.

Gent's Furnishings

OF LATEST STYLES

In Endless Variety!

MINERS' WEAR

OF BEST MAKES

AND DURABLE QUALITY.

BOOTS AND SHOES MADE TO ORDER.
SHIRTS MADE TO ORDER.
SUITS MADE TO ORDER.
ALL WARRANTED TO FIT.

☞No Trouble to Show You Goods. Call and Examine Our Stock.

☞We have ONE PRICE and will give you satisfaction.

CHAS. GLOVER & CO.

The Boss Furnishers.

July 22, 1880

R. F. HAFFORD & CO.,

WHOLESALE AND RETAIL DEALERS IN IMPORTED AND DOMESTIC

Wines, Liquors and Cigars.

ALLEN STREET, NEAR FOURTH, TOMBSTONE, ARIZONA.

Whiskies:

Old Kentucky
Old Reserve,
Our Choice,
Coronet,
Log Cabin, No. 1
O. K. Cutter and Miller's
Chicken Cock and Rye.

Brandies:

Hennessy, Martell and other noted Brands.

Gin:

Holland, Keynard Old Tom Rums, etc. Keep constantly on hand the best of WINES and CIGARS Imported and Dom

McKEAN & KNIGHT,

Wholesale and Retail Dealers in

GENERAL MERCHANDISE.

CORNER SIXTH AND ALLEN STREETS,

Tombstone, Arizona.

M. CALISHER & CO.,

Wholesale and Retail

DEALERS IN GENERAL MERCHANDISE.

Also, Lumber and Building Material.

ALLEN STREET, TOMBSTONE, BETWEEN 5TH AND 6TH.

JOSEPH HOEFLER,

Dealer in GENERAL MERCHANDISE

ALLEN STREET, TOMBSTONE.

November 8, 1880

The Custom Mill.

From Superintendent Emanuel, of the Vizina, we learn that the Boston mill has started on the 1,000 tons of ore which they have contracted to work, but, owing to the upset, which we noticed Tuesday, they were obliged to "hang up" the stamps yesterday. Superintendent Rice has just put in new scales for weighing the ore, which are now ready for use. Indications now point to a very successful operation of the new mill, with its corresponding great benefits to the camp.

Overtaken by Justice.

Deputy Sheriff Earp on Sunday evening last arrested James Langdon, alias Red Mike, on the charge of murdering one Leonard in Virginia City, Nevada, about a year ago. Red Mike was arrested at the time of the murder, but managed to break jail prior to his trial. The killing was done with a bowie knife, and is said to have been entirely unprovoked. When arrested, Mike was standing in front of Danner & Owen's saloon. Upon making the arrest, Earp said to him: "I suppose you know what this is for?" Mike replied in the affirmative, and made no effort at resistance. He was lodged in jail to await the arrival of a Nevada officer with a requisition.

November 8, 1880

Marshal White's Funeral.

The circumstances attending the death of Fred White, Marshal of Tombstone, who was murdered in the discharge of his duty, called out the largest assemblage which has ever followed to the tomb any deceased person in Tombstone. The funeral services were held in Gird's Hall and long ere the hour for the funeral services the spacious building was crowded to its utmost capacity. Rev. Mr. McIntyre preached the funeral sermon, and took occasion to indulge in a speculative philosophy of the great unknown, of which he is as ignorant as the babe unborn. To say that the reverened gentleman trenched upon the bounds of common sense is but to echo the sentiment of the vast congregation who had assembled to listen to a funeral sermon and not to hear a dessertation on speculation, would be but stating the exact truth. The reverend knows just as much about the Great Unknown as any living creature who has never been there, and his captious flings at the firemen's resolutions were as injudicious as they were ill-timed. The cortege following the murdered Marshal to the grave was the largest ever seen in our embryo city. It embraced all classes and conditions of society, from the millionaire to the mudsill and numbered fully 1,000 persons.

Another Murder.

A teamster from the railroad reports the finding of the body of a man in a ravine near Benson. The body had probably lain where found for about three weeks, and was much disfigured and wasted. The teeth and skull were broken in and a bullet had entered the brain just behind the eye. Several heavy stones were lying near the body, and all circumstances point to a foul crime. The body is believed to be that of a man who disappeared from Benson about three weeks since, and his assassin is supposed to be a Mexican who has probably crossed into Sonora. The name of the murdered man was mentioned, but has escaped us.

Prospector
February 04, 1890

SAVE YOUR MONEY!

BY GETTING YOUR TINNING, PLUMBING AND SHEET IRON WORK DONE AT THE

CASH TIN SHOP!

Sixth Street, Between Allen and Fremont.

W. FESENFELD, Manager.

☞Hotel and Restaurant Work a Specialty. ROOFING and Jobbing of the Best Material aud Workmanship at the Lowest Price. TINWARE, Stoves and Housefurnishing Goods. WATERPIPES and FITTINGS, all sizes. Estimates furnished for anything in the above line at bottom figures. Give me a call.

TOBACCO, CIGARS, ETC.

I. LEVI & CO.,

IMPORTERS AND DEALERS IN

Havana Cigars and Tobaccos,

Books and Stationery,

Pipes, Cutlery, Musical Instruments, Notions,

Fancy Goods, Etc., Etc.

Allen St., Below Fifth

Arcade Cigar, Tobacco and Notion Store,

A. COHN & BRO., PROPRIETORS.

JUST OPENED, with the **FINEST** and **BEST SELECTED STOCK** of all the Favorite Brands of **IMPORTED** and **DOMESTIC CIGARS, TOBACCO, STATIONERY, CUTLERY**, and a general assortment of Smokers' Articles and Yankee Notions, all of which we propose to sell at Lowest Possible Rates.

☞Dealers will save money by ascertaining our prices before sending their orders elsewhere. Special attention is called to our line of Meershaum and Amber goods. County orders promptly attended to.

A. COHN & BRO.,

ALLEN STREET, JOINING ARCADE RESTAURANT, TOMBSTONE.

Blanks at this Office.

FURNITURE.

LEO GOLDSCHMIDT,

DEALER IN

FURNITURE, CARPETS & BEDDING

FOURTH STREET, OPPOSITE POST OFFICE, TOMBSTONE.

J. L. FONCK, MANAGER.

Largest and Most Complete Assortment of Furniture Arizona. Orders will Receive Prompt Attention.

The Alhambra.

T. N. CORRIGAN, - - Proprieto

Elegantly re-fitted and just re-opened with the finest stock of **Wines, Liquors** and **Cigars** ever brought to Tombstone.

My stock embraces the famous **O. K., Cutter, Hermitage, Old Government** and **Stonewall** brands. Imported Brandies. My wines and liquors have been especially selected for the Tombstone trade and can not be surpassed for age and bouquet. **Cigars** were made to order and of the choicest Havana tobacco.

The Old Boys are notified that the Latch String is always the outside

R. COHEN,

THE LARGEST AND CHEAPEST STORE IN TOMBSTON

FREMONT STREET, NEAR SIXTH.

GROCERIES, PROVISIONS,
LIQUORS, TOBACCO,
HARDWARE, CROCKERY,
MINING AND MILL SUPPLIES, OILS, PAINTS,
BLACKSMITH and CARPENTER TOOLS,
BOOTS, CLOTHING, HATS, BEDDING, ETC., ET

Which Will Be Sold at the LOWEST CASH RATES.

PLUMBING AND STEAM-FITTING.

T. A. Atchison,

Pioneer Plumber and Steam Fitte

FOURTH STREET, TOMBSTONE,
Three Doors Above POST OFFICE.

☞ Having conducted this line of business for years in the States, and essing a Complete Outfit of Machinery and Tools, I am prepared to do work in this line in the best manner possible.

ROOFING A SPECIALTY.

Orders Filled Promptly and LOW for Cash. Stoves, Granite Ware, Tinwa Wire, Etc., and all Miners' Outfits constantly on hand.

GRAND HOTEL.

GRAND HOTEL

Just Opened,

ALLEN STREET, TOMBSTONE.

The Finest Hotel in Arizona.

Regular Board, $9 per week. Single Meals, 50 cen

BEDS, $1 PER NIGHT.

UNION NEWS DEPOT.

GRAND OPENING!

THE UNION NEWS DEPOT

Has Just RECEIVED the First Shipment of NEW and SELECTED STOCK

Staple and Fancy Stationery,
School Books, Cigars, Tobaccos, etc.

Call and examine before purchasing elsewhere. FOURTH STREET, Ne Door to Post Office.

SOLOMON ISRAEL, Proprietor.

MARK P. SHAFFER. FRANK E. LORD.

SHAFFER & LORD.

COMMISSION-MERCHANTS AND DEALERS IN GENERAL MERCHANDISE,

CORNER FREMONT AND FIFTH STREETS.

THE ORIGINAL

Miners and Prospectors Store.

Established Before any other now in Town

Having facilities for securing goods at the lowest figures, we are now prepared to sell at lower prices than any other firm and will receive adobe dollars at par from cash purchasers.

Groceries and Provisions.

COAL OIL

September 28, 1880

THE COSMOPOLITAN,

ALLEN STREET, TOMBSTONE, A.

The Largest and Best Hotel in the District.

Headquarters for All Stage Companies.

9-28-80 C. BILICKE, Proprietor.

July 22, 1882

New Cosmopolitan Hotel.

Owing to the impossibility of accommodating the large and rapidly increasing custom of the Cosmopolitan Hotel, Mr. Bilicke has recently purchased the vacant lot opposite, from Mr. Pierce, and will begin at once the erection of a large two-story building for hotel purposes. The edifice will be 120x20 feet on the ground. But two stories will be put up at present; the walls, however, will be constructed to receive a third story, if necessary. The front of the lower story will be occupied as a store, and the remainder of the building divided into fifty sleeping apartments. When completed, it will be furnished in a manner befitting the style of building, which Mr. Bilicke informs us will outvie any hotel yet erected in Tombstone.

The Oriental Saloon opened up yesterday morning as fresh and bright as a daisy. Old age don't put a single wrinkle on the brow of the Oriental, which under the influence (lady like) of a new complexion, always keeps young. Joyce had his popular establishment completely renovated and painted, besides having secured the finest lot of pictures to be found in any public house in the Territory. The character of the goods behind the bar is too well established to need mention.

July 22, 1880

The Oriental.

For several weeks past the spacious corner building of the Vizina & Cook Block has been undergoing numerous finishing touches preparatory to its occupation by Messrs. M. E. Joyce & Co., the genial proprietors of the soon-to-be famous Oriental. Last evening the portals were thrown open and the public permitted to gaze upon the most elegantly furnished saloon this side of the favored city of the Golden Gate. Twenty-eight burners suspended in neat chandeliers afforded an illumination of ample brilliancy, and the bright rays reflected from the many colored crystals on the bar sparkled like a December iceling in the sunshine. The saloon comprises two apartments. To the right of the main entrance is the bar, beautifully carved, finished in white and gilt and capped with a handsomely polished top. In the rear of this stand a brace of side-boards which are simply elegant and must be seen to be appreciated. They were made for the Baldwin Hotel, of San Francisco, but being too small Mr. Joyce purchased them. The back apartment is covered with a brilliant body brussels carpet, and suitably furnished after the style of a grand club room, with conveniences for the wily dealers in polished ivory. The selection of the furniture and fixtures displays an exquisite taste, and nothing seems to have been forgotten—even to a handsome stock of stationary. Tombstone takes the lead and Messrs. Joyce & Co. our congratulations.

STILL ON DECK.

THAT OLD AND POPULAR RESORT. THE

ORIENTAL.

Continues to supply its numerous Patrons with the Purest Brands of

WHISKIES, BRANDIES, WINES,
ALES, BEERS, ETC., ETC.

And the choicest selection of Cigars ever brought to this city.

M. E. JOYCE, - - Proprietor.

The Alhambra.

T. N. CORRIGAN, - - Proprieto[r]

Elegantly re-fitted and just re-opened with the finest stock of **Wines, Liquors and Cigars** ever brought to Tombstone.

My stock embraces the famous **O. K., Cutter, Hermitage, Old Government** and **Stonewall** brands. Imported Brandies. My wines and liquors have been especially selected for the Tombstone trade and can not be surpassed for age and bouquet. **Cigars** were made to order and of the choicest Havana tobacco.

The Old Boys are notified that the Latch String is always [on] the outside

September 28, 1880

R. COHEN,

THE LARGEST AND CHEAPEST STORE IN TOMBSTON[E]

FREMONT STREET, NEAR SIXTH.

GROCERIES, PROVISIONS,
LIQUORS, TOBACCO,
HARDWARE, CROCKERY,
MINING AND MILL SUPPLIES, OILS, PAINTS,
BLACKSMITH and CARPENTER TOOLS,
BOOTS, CLOTHING, HATS, BEDDING, ETC., E[TC.]

Which Will Be Sold at the LOWEST CASH RATES.

TOBACCO, CIGARS, ETC.

I. LEVI & CO.,

IMPORTERS AND DEALERS IN

Havana Cigars and Tobaccos,

TOMBSTONE DAILY EPITAPH, SEPTEMBER 28, 1880.

GUNSMITHING.

HART'S GUN SHOP,

SIGN OF THE BIG REVOLVER AND KEY, FREMONT ST.,

Is the place to get all kinds of GUN WORK done in a workmanlike manner and warranted. Locks repaired and keys fitted, Engraving, Wood and Iron turning, and repairs on anything done on short notice. S. L. HART.

The Other "ONLY" Complete Repairing Outfit in the Territory.

TINWARE PLUMBING ETC.

WATERMAN & GOODRICH,

DEALERS IN

Stoves and Ranges of all Kinds

TIN WARE, SHEET IRON and COPPER WARE on hand or made to order. All kinds of Job Work and repairing on shortest notice by experienced workmen. Call and find all kinds of House Furnishing Goods after failing elsewhere. Terms moderate for currency or U. S. coin. Orders from the country attended to as punctually as for the town.

Fredericks & Hill's Tin Shop,

Allen Street, Tombstone.

Sheet Iron and Jobber Work! Roofing and Jobbing of Every Description at the Lowest Possible Prices. Tinware: Milk Pans, Granite Ware and Cooking Stoves, etc. sold CHEAPER than any other place in Tombstone. Be sure to call before buying elsewhere. Plumbing, Gas and Steam Fitting Done by Competent Workmen.

SAVE YOUR MONEY!

BY GETTING YOUR TINNING, PLUMBING AND SHEET IRON WORK DONE AT THE

CASH TIN SHOP!

Sixth Street, Between Allen and Fremont.

W. FESENFELD, Manager.

☞Hotel and Restaurant Work a Specialty. ROOFING and Jobbing of the Best Material aud Workmanship at the Lowest Price. TINWARE, Stoves and Housefurnishing Goods. WATERPIPES and FITTINGS, all sizes. Estimates furnished for anything in the above line at bottom figures. Give me a call.

John P. Clum, Mayor
Postmaster of Tombstone
Editor of the Epitaph

MAYOR'S MESSAGE.

Mayor Declares Tombstone In Need Of Jail, Ordinances To Control City.

Daily Nugget, Jan. 13, 1881.

Message of the New Mayor.

Following is the text of the Mayor's message to the new council:

Gentlemen: It did not occur to me until yesterday afternoon that the usages of such occasions would expect from the new executive a formal expression of his views and recommendations concerning the administration of affairs now entrusted to this body. I regret that I was not reminded of this custom earlier, as I would gladly have devoted more time and thought to the consideration of our present necessities than has been possible for me to do in the brief period since taking the oath of office.

I enter upon the duties of my office not only with a feeling of pride, but also with a desire and a determination to know and to perform my duty to the best of my ability. My regret is therefore sincere that this, my first duty, could not have been performed with greater completeness and mutual satisfaction.

FIRMNESS NECESSARY.

We have entered upon an administration of unusual importance, and the record of this year's events will, in my opinion, form no ordinary part of the history of the City of Tombstone. Matters of greatest moment to individuals and to the community will be submitted for our deliberation and action. We were chosen for the respective positions we occupy because the public have confidence in our integrity, fair purpose and good judgment. If we, in the conduct of municipal affairs, tolerate without objection aught that does not harmonize with our best judgment and sense of right, we betray the trust reposed in us by our constituents. If the performance of our duty is characterized by indifference and neglect, we shall prove ourselves unworthy of public confidence and esteem. Our purpose will, therefore, be to employ such wisdom, discretion and firmness as will command the respect and approbation of the community and perpetuate mutual confidence and good feeling.

It is perhaps unnecessary to outline the policy I would suggest, except in the general terms above expressed. The rapid growth of the city will constantly change the necessities of the situation, and our deliberations must at all times be controlled by the requirements or exigencies of the moment.

NO CITY CHARTER.

I am informed that no application has ever been made for a charter for the city of Tombstone—an instrument which, under the laws of our Territory, is constituted a legal necessity. We should therefore see to it that the proper application is made at once. This, as well as other legal documents, must be framed with understanding and care. I would therefore deem it advisable to employ at once a competent and reliable city attorney. Too much caution cannot be exercised in the selection of this official, as the council will have frequent occasion to seek his advice during the present year.

In the nature of social affairs, it is impossible to maintain any organization without funds. Our city treasury is alarmingly void of the needful cash. Therefore the sources of revenue from which the corporation is to derive its support becomes a subject of first consideration with us. I shall suggest a committee on finance, who may give immediate attention to the collection of licenses, fines, taxes and other revenues justly due the city.

UNFORTUNATE EVENTS.

In this connection I may direct attention to the vacant lots which are at the present time, by a series of unfortunate events, tied up in the courts. I deem it a paramount duty with us to use every endeavor to regain the title and benefits of these lots, in order that the community may enjoy the considerable proceeds resulting from the sale or rent thereof. This subject should, in my judgment, be submitted to the committee on finance for consideration and report.

I am informed that there exists no official map of the town. This is a matter of importance, and suggests the necessity of a committee on streets, surveys, water for fire purposes, etc. This committee will undoubtedly report the necessity for the employment of a city surveyor, and make such other recommendations as the necessities of the situation and the limited revenues of the town will permit.

The question of deeds to city property and occupied by citizens, is perhaps the most delicate and complicated subject to be disposed of by this body. We cannot employ too much caution in the execution of our trusts in these matters.

PEACE IMPORTANT.

The peace and good of our city is a most important consideration which cannot be overlooked or neglected. In all frontier towns there are various disturbing elements which must be restrained and controlled. To this end an efficient police force must be maintained, and a suitable jail should be at once provided. Several new ordinances will be found essential for the direction of the city marshal and the proper organization of our public system.

Tombstone is largely made up of buildings of combustible materials. We stand in constant danger of serious loss and disaster from destroying flames. It will therefore be an important duty as the corporate body of the community, to make such suggestions and pass such ordinances as will most efficiently protect our city from destruction through the agency of this fierce element.

OPINIONS DESIRED.

Other matters, equal in importance to this already mentioned, will present themselves as we convene from time to time in our official capacity. Upon these questions each should feel it a privilege and duty to express positive opinions. While these opinions may differ, our motives will not be misinterpreted. Such expressions are essential to the end we seek to attain.

There is little satisfaction in life except in duty faithfully performed, with the realization of good results appreciated by those we seek to benefit. Let us endeavor to act upon these principles and we cannot fail to leave a record no one need be ashamed of.

JOHN P. CLUM,
Mayor.

Tombstone, January 12, 1881.

Arrested

(From the Tombstone Epitaph)

Augustine Martinez and "Dutch Annie," a couple of soiled doves, were arrested last night on charges of using indecent language. The trial of the first mentioned will take place in court this morning, while Annie will put in an appearance before Justice Shearer at 3 o'clock this afternoon.

(Daily Epitaph)
(Sept. 3, 1881)

LAST night was perfectly lovely, and, as a fine team dashed by, the society reporter observed that if it did not rain to-morrow evening he thought he would take a ride too. We are afraid, however, that it will.

THE EMERALD has commenced to ship ore to the Boston Mill. It is not known how much they intend having worked at this time, but probably no great quantity, as the mine has not been opened out for regular shipments at present.

THE SUIT that has been hanging over the Silver Belt, Banner, Standard and Huron mines, has been amicably settled by Messrs. Williams and Ogden, parties thereto. Work on the Silver Belt will start up next week and will be vigorously pushed until a development of ore is reached.

Deputy Appointed By Sheriff Behan

(Epitaph, Sept. 3, 1881)

SHERIFF BEHAN has appointed Police Officer Bronk a special deputy for Tombstone. This is a good and wise appointment, as it gives the Police Officer, Bronk, jurisdiction outside the city limits in the case of an offender making for the Tough Nut side of town, where many fly for safety.

Let Justice be Done

(Daily Epitaph)
(Sept. 3, 1881)

It having been rumored and reported that the Secretary of Rescue Hook and Ladder Company was in default in payment of funds to the treasurer of the company, it is proper that his explanation should have the same circulation as the report, as we love justice—or as our forefathers had it—"Fiat justicia rua eoelum."

Mr. Ross claims that it was his duty to pay over these funds solely at a regular meeting; that had he done otherwise he would have been responsible for a second payment. This is a point we have no voice in deciding. If there is a fair room for question on the proposition, then this young man should not be condemned. Evidently, from the fact of his paying over the money as soon as he was advised so to do, as his proper course, demonstrates that there could be no evil intent in his part.

Justicia.

It gives us pleasure to have an opportunity to publish this.

Tombstone Well In

(Epitaph, Sept. 3, 1881)

THE TOMBSTONE WATER, Mill & Lumber Company is making rapid progress at the well. Thursday they struck a new vein of water that came in with a rush, and at the rate of six thousand gallons an hour. This give an assurance of a lasting and abundant supply. The material for the reservoir is nearly all on the ground, and the pipe is expected to arrive to-day. The ditch has all been cleared out and pipe laying will commence the moment it begins to arrive. If the present fine weather continues thirty or forty days will see water flowing into the city from this source.

May 26, 1881

AMAZON BOURBON WHISKY

Kentucky's Finest Production.

P. W. SMITH,
COR. FOURTH AND ALLEN STS.
TOMBSTONE, ARIZONA.

Agent for the
Amazon Distilling Comp'y,
OF COVINGTON, KY.

R. F. HAFFORD & CO.,

WHOLESALE AND RETAIL DEALERS IN IMPORTED AND DOMESTIC

Wines, Liquors and Cigars,

Corner Allen and Fourth, - - - Tombstone.

July 3, 1881

FURNITURE.

FURNITURE.

J. LENOIR,

—DEALER IN—

CARPETS and BEDDING.

308 Allen Street **Near Third.**

The Largest and Most Complete assortment of Eastern and California Furniture ever brought to Arizona. You will find it to your advantage to examine my Stock before Purchasing elsewhere.

A. J. RITTER W. H. REAM.

RITTER & REAM,

City Undertakers.

HAVE ON HAND A GOOD SUPPLY OF COFFINS, CASES, TRIMMINGS AND ROBES FOR Ladies and gentlemen. Also, zinc-lined cases for shipping bodies. Having had long experience for the business, we think we can give satisfaction. We are prepared to do anything in the line of jobbing, repairing furniture, making desks, bookcases, tables, and setting-up, leveling and repairing billiard tables. All work guaranteed. **613** Allen street.

"Apache Devil" Lost His Head

(From the Tombstone Epitaph)

Gon-Sha, the Apache devil who murdered Billy Diehl a little over two years ago, now lies with several feet of dirt over him at the Territorial prison cemetery minus his head. After hanging himself last Thursday in his cell he was buried, but the night following some scientific cuss went to the burying ground, dug him up and cut off his head, and left no clue where the missing cranium can be found.

TRAIN ROBBERY.

Epitaph, 1881.

Train Number seventeen was held up by three masked men Wednesday night near Pantano. The men compelled the engineer to stop the train. When the Express messenger refused to open the door, the robbers threw in half a dozen bombs and forced their way in. The safe was robbed. The robbers escaped on horseback. The messenger's ribs were broken. The company has offered $1,000 each for their apprehension.

DASTARDLY DEED.

Epitaph, 1881.

The following report received from Tucson at nine o'clock last evening from Sheriff Shibell at Pantano says, "We took the trail of the robbers and followed it about a mile east of Mountain Springs, where we ran the trail into a cave where the robbers had been residing for some time back. We found a half dozen cans of coffee, sugar, dried beef and other articles of cooking. We are unable to find any trail leading out of the mountains. It is necessary to have a couple of good Indian trailers.

Silver Flake Floods

(Daily Epitaph)

(December 14, 1881)

It is but a few days since we announced the starting up afresh of the Silver Flake mine, and we had hoped to have included it in our weekly reports; but the elements, it seems were against this desirable end, for we have been informed by the superintendent that water has been struck at fifty-two feet depth in such abundance that it cannot be controlled by hand. At no other point near Tombstone has water been struck at so slight a depth. In the Silver Bell at 190 feet. The locality of the Silver Flake is such that a less depth might reasonably be expected to develop water, it being on the rolling mesa between the Owl's Nest and Pickem Up Station. The ledge, it is said, was showing finely, and the assays were showing a better class of ore with every foot attained in depth. Mr. Gerrold, the superintendent, will leave for San Francisco shortly where machinery will be obtained to continue the work of development.

GUN FIGHT.

Three Die In Minute At OK Corral.

Epitaph, October 27, 1881.

Tombstone, Oct. 26, 1881 – The liveliest street battle that ever occurred in Tombstone took place at 2:30 p.m. to-day, resulting in the death of three persons, one probably fatally. For some time past several cowboys have been in town, and the fight was between the city marshal, Virgil Earp, his two brothers, Morgan and Wyatt Earp and Doc Holliday on one side, and Ike and Billy Clanton and Frank and Tom McLowry on the other.

The Clantons and McLowery brothers are known as cowboys, and Ike has been in town for the past week drinking pretty freely, and was arrested this morning for carrying concealed weapons, he having appeared on the street with a Winchester rifle and a six] shooter on. After paying his fine he is reported to have made threats against Marshal Earp and his brothers, and it is known that bad blood existed between them for some time.

About 2:30 o'clock the marshal requested his brothers, Morgan and Wyatt and Doc Holliday to accompany him to aid in disarming the cowboys, as trouble was feared in the evening. They started toward the O.K. Corral on Fremont street, and a few doors below the Nugget office saw the Clantons and the McLowery brothers talking to Sheriff Behan, who had requested them to disarm. The marshal called out, "Boys, throw up your hands; I want you to give up your shooters."

30 SHOTS IN A MINUTE.

At this Frank McLowery attempted to draw his pistol, when Wyatt Earp immediately shot him, the ball entering just about the waist. Doc Holliday then let go at Tom McLowery with a shotgun, filling him full of buckshot under the right arm. Billy Clanton then blazed away at Marshal Earp, and Ike Clanton, who it is claimed was unarmed, started and ran off through the corral to Allen street. The firing then became general, and some thirty shots were fired, all in such rapid succession that the fight was over in less than a minute.

When the smoke cleared away it was found that Frank McLowery had been killed outright, with one ball through the torso, one in the left breast, and one in the right temple, the latter two wounds being received at the same instant. Tom McLowery lay dead around the corner of Third street, a few feet from Fremont, the load of buckshot fired by Holliday killing him almost instantly. Billy Clanton lay on the side of the street, with one shot in the right waist and another in the right side near the wrist, and the third in the left breast. He was taken into a house and lived about half an hour in great agony.

INJURIES OF THE WOUNDED.

Morgan Earp was shot through both shoulders, the ball creasing the skin, Marshal Earp was shot through the fleshy part of the right leg. Wyatt Earp and Doc Holliday escaped unhurt.

The shooting created great excitement and the streets was immediately filled with people. Ike Clanton was captured and taken to jail where he now remains. The jail is guarded by a number of citizens to prevent lynching, of which there is no apparent danger. The three dead bodies were removed to the morgue, where they now lie.

It is reported that several thousand dollars were found on the bodies. The feeling of the better class citizens is that the marshal and his possee acted solely in the right in attempting to disarm the cowboys, and that it was a case of kill or get killed. Clanton's father was killed with four others a few months ago in New Mexico by the Mexicans while driving a band of cattle up to this market. The town is quiet and the authorities are fully able to maintain order.

CORONER'S VERDICT.

Tombstone (A.T.) Oct. 31, 1881 – The coroner's jury, after deliberating for two hours in regard to the late killing of William Clanton, Frank and Tom McLowery, brought in a verdict that the men named came to their deaths in the town of Tombstone on October 26, 1881, from the effect of pistol and gun shot wounds inflicted by Virgil Earp, Morgan Earp, Wyatt Earp, and the Holliday, commony called 'Doc' Holliday." The verdict does not seem to meet with general approval, as it does not state whether the cowboys were killed by the marshal and his party in the discharge of their duty, or whether the killing was justifiable.

On Saturday, warrants for the arrest of Wyatt, Virgil and Morgan Earp and J.H. (Doc) Holliday were placed in the hands of the sheriff, but as Morgan and Virgil Earp were confined to their beds through wounds received in the late street fight, the warrants were not in their cases served, and only Wyatt Earp and Holliday were placed under arrest. When these parties were taken before Justice Spicer he at first denied bail, but upon showing of the facts by affidavits, bail was granted and fixed in the sum of $10,000 each, being justified in the sume of $20,000 for each of the defendants, which amount was furnished.

Today Holliday and Wyatt Earp were before Justice Spicer to answer the charge. The investigation was conducted with closed doors. No one, excepting the officers of the court and the witnesses whose testmony was being taken up, were allowe inside. The investigation is not yet concluded and will probably occupy the court for several days.

(Tombstone Democrat, Jan. 9, 1886)

Despise no small thing. A little nip will often brace up a big man.

Tucson, Nov. 1 – It was reported today that the marshal of Tombstone had telegraphed for troops to protect the town from an attack of cowboy friends of the late murdered cowboys. Later advices say there is no truth in the report of trouble and no need for the call for troops. Everything is quiet in town and the investigation is proceeding by closed doors. Under statutory rules none of the testimony is allowed to be published. There is more assured feeling of security now than since the shooting. The friends of the murdered cowboys will fight it out in court without resorting to any bloodshed.

Mayor John P. Clum Feared Lost in Attack on Stage Coach But Found Uninjured in Benson After Party Searches All Night

Tombstone Epitaph
Dec. 15, 1881

The announcement in yesterday's Epitaph of the attacks upon the coach night before last threw the city into wildest excitement, and the gravest apprehensions were felt for Mayor Clum. As before stated, upon receipt of the news a party started out about 3 a.m. to obtain some tidings of the missing mayor among whom were Sheriff Behan and C .D. Reppy. The sheriff and Mr. Reppy started first and arrived at Contention between 4 and 5 o'clock, where they learned from Mr. Danham, of Philadelphia, who was on the stage, the first particulars of the affair. The six-horse coach, driven by Jimmy Harrington, and the bullion wagon, driven by "Whistling Dick" had just left Malcolm's water station which is the last house on the road to Contention, and only about four miles from Tombstone, and were bowling along at a rapid gait, when the order to "Halt!" given from the roadside, and almost simultaneously a volley was fired into them. The off-leader of the coach was struck in the neck, and all the horses became unmanageable. Dick was hit in the calf of the leg, receiving a painful flesh wound, but kept his seat and his wagon right side up. The horses ran about half a mile when the wounded and weakened one fell from loss of blood. Mr. Clum, with the assistance of other passengers, cut the leader loose, and on they went, it being the general impression all the passengers were aboard. Mr. Clum had been riding on the inside and he was missed, but it was supposed by his fellow passengers that he had taken a seat on the outside, consequently, his absence was not detected until the arrival of the coach at Contention. Upon learning this, Messrs. Behan and Reppy started for Tombstone and upon arriving at the place where the attack was made, examined the locality carefully, but no trace of the missing man was found. In the meantime

THE SECOND PARTY

which had left Tombstone about 8 a.m. upon arriving at Malcolm's Station, learned that two teamsters in camp with their wagons at that point, had not only heard the noise of their shooting, but could distinctly see the flash, the attack having been made about the apex of the first rise beyond. Continuing down the road about a half-mile beyond the attacking point by the light of a match, two large pools of blood were found on the right, where the leader had given out, and after wandering several hundred rods to the right of the right of the road, marking his trail by his ebbing life, had already fallen prey to a skulking coyote. Not being able to discover any trail, the party proceeded on to Contention, where from Mr. Dunham it was learned that after assisting in releasing the wounded leader, it was supposed by the passengers that Mr. Clum had either taken a seat with the driver in the bullion wagon, while it was rationally presented by the driver that he was inside, and his absence was not ascertained until arriving at Contention. Just after leaving Mr. Dunham it was stated that Mr. C. had been heard of at the Grand Central Mill, whither the party proceeded, and learned that the mayor had taken the ore road to the mill, from whence, after resting, he had gone by saddle to Benson, arriving between 7 and 8 o'clock.

As the temasters at Malcolm's and Mr. Dunham both stated that the flashes seemed to come from both sides of the road, and as the wound received by the bullion driver, as well as the death-shot to a faithful leader that had done service ever since the establishment of the line, were made by revolvers, it does not, to say the least, give the semblance of an organized intent to rob the stage, as no rifle cartridge shells could be found on the ground, and all parties claim that there were from 15 to 20 shots fired in quick succession.

From Mr. O'Brien, one of the teamsters, it was learned that the would-be murderers had probably taken up the gulch to the northeast, just above Malcolm's, as about one hundred yards from the road there is evidence of the repeated hitching of horses in the thick brush, and shortly after the shooting the sound of flying hoofs came from that direction.

Whether this affair was a brutal attempt at assassination or a bungling effort to rob the stage, the passengers and drivers had a narrow escape from death amidst the whistling robbers and it is hardly presumable that the most ignorant Hottentot or brutal Apache would be as callous and unjust, as to attempt to ridicule any person who was upon the coach. This was reserved, but yesterday morning's Nugget, and where and when this is said the utmost dregs of possibility have been reached.

October 27, 1881

4-PAW'S

Monster Railroad Circus, Museum, Menagerie

—— AND ——

ELEVATED STAGE !

Just Stupendiously Reinforced With

Samwell's Trained Animal Exposition,

Coming on their own Special train of Cars to

Fairbank, Tuesday.

EMPRESS,

The $10,000 largest Performing Elephant in the world.

TWENTY-FIVE

English Grey-hounds, Champion Leapers and Runners of America.

TWENTY-FIVE

Trained Shetland Ponies, the Smallest on Earth.

Trained Stallions !

Riding Dogs !

Riding Goats !

Riding Monkeys !

Performing Bears !

Performing Den of Lions !

MILLE ZOLA, Queen of the Air, Ri ing a Bicyole Fifty Feet High on a Slender Wire Blind-folded.

MILLE ANNIE, the only Lady Back and Forward Bender.

MISS ANNIE FOREPAUGH, the Youngest Lady Bareback Rider in America.

One hundred New and Novel Features all takes place in one Old-fashioned Ring and Elevated Stage.

Look out for the Monster Free Street Parade at 11 a. m. Door open at 1 and 7 p. m. Performance an hour later. Remember the day and date.

March 16, 1881

HOLD!

Eight Road Agents Attempt to Stop Kinnear's Stage.

The Terrible "Hold!" Followed by a Volley!

"Budd," the Driver, and One Passenger Killed.

A Good Man Gone to Meet His Maker.

Brave Bob Paul on Deck as Usual.

He Answers the Robbers Shot for Shot.

Contention City, Tombstone and Benson Aroused.

Three Bands of Armed Men After the Robbers.

Probability that They Will be Soon Captured.

At about 11 o'clock last night, Marshal Williams received a telegram from Benson stating that Kinnear & Company's coach, carrying Wells Fargo & Co.'s treasure, had been stopped near Contention and "Budd" Philpot, the driver, killed and one passenger mortally wounded. Almost immediately afterward A. C. Cowan, Wells Fargo & Co.'s agent at Contention City, rode into this city, bringing a portion of the details of the affair. In a few minutes after his arrival, Williams, the Earp brothers, and several other brave, determined men were in the saddle, well armed, en route to the scene of the murderous affray. From telegrams received from Benson at the EPITAPH office, the following particulars of the affair were gathered:

As the stage was going up a small incline about two hundred yards this side of Drew's Station and about a mile the other side of Contention City, a man stepped into the road from the east side and called out "Hold!" At the same moment a number of men—believed to have been eight—made their appearance, and a shot was fired from the same side of the road, instantly followed by another. One of these shots struck "Budd" Philpot, the driver, who fell heavily forward between the wheelers, carrying the reins with him. The horses immediately sprang into a dead run. Meanwhile, Bob Paul, Wells, Fargo & Co's messenger, one of the bravest and coolest men who ever sat on a box-seat, was ready with his gun and answered back shot for shot before the frightened horses had whirled the coach out of range. It was fully a mile before the team could be brought to a stand, when it was discovered that one of the shots had mortally wounded a passenger on the coach named Peter Roering. As soon as the coach could be stopped, Paul secured the reins and drove rapidly to Benson, and immediately started back for the scene of the murder. At Benson a telegram was sent to the EPITAPH office, stating that Roering could not possibly live. There were eight passengers on the coach, and they all united in praise of Mr. Paul's bravery and presence of mind.

At Drew's Station the firing and rapid whirling by of the coach sent the men at the station to the scene of the tragedy, when they found poor "Budd" lying dead in the road, and by the bright moonlight saw the murderers fleeing rapidly from the place. A messenger was at once dispatched to inform agent Cowan of the circumstances, and within twenty minutes after the news arrived Mr. Cowan had despatched nearly thirty well-armed volunteers after the scoundrels. He then rode rapidly into Tombstone, when the party above mentioned started out to aid in the pursuit. This, with Mr. Paul's party, makes three bodies of determined men who are in hot chase, and Mr. Cowan stated to an EPITAPH reporter that it is almost impossible for the murderous gang to escape, as the pursuers are close at their heels and have the moonlight in their favor. Should the road-agents be caught they will meet with the short shift which they deserve.

"Budd," the murdered driver, whose real name is Eli Philpot, was one of the most widely known stage-drivers on the Coast. For years he has borne a high reputation as a skillful handler of the "ribbons," won on the principal stage lines in California, and during a year's residence in Arizona, most of the latter time in the employ of Kinnear's (formerly Walker & Co's.) line. He will be sincerely mourned, not only by hosts of personal friends, but by thousands of passengers who have ridden on the box-seat with him and been captivated by his simple manners and frank, manly ways. It was a rare treat to "make the trip" with him, for his memory was rich in reminiscences of the "old stage days" in California, and when he so willed he could keep a companion's attention riveted by his quaint, droll conversation. He has a wife and young family at Calistoga, California, who had the tenderest place in his big heart. And now there is another little home in the world which has been desolated and despoiled by the ruthless bullet. There is something inexpressibly sad in the sudden death of such outwardly rough, but inwardly brave, true-hearted men, and no better representation of this class could be found than the man whom the murderers last night sent unwarned to his last home. He was as proud and fond of his team and the big new coach on which he met his death as if they were human, and the horses always seemed to know when "Budd" was at the other end of the lines.

"Budd" has had a presentment of coming evil ever since the night, a short time ago, when the stage was stopped between Tombstone and Contention, and a bullet sent whizzing between him and Jack Allman. The latter gentleman, between whom and "Bud" a strong friendship existed, states that only on Monday morning last he mailed for his friend a long and loving letter to the dear ones at home. But before the missive reaches its destination the wires will have borne the crushing intelligence that will cause the bitterest of all human heart-aches.

Jack, who is agent for Kinnear & Co., probably had himself a narrow escape, from the fact that his usual place with the coach was behind "Budd" on the upper box seat, and the only reason why he was not there last night was the fact that the withdrawal of an opposition stage line made unnecessary his nightly trip to Benson.

Arcade Restaurant ! !

MISS NELLIE CASHMAN, Proprtr'ss.

AGAIN AT MY OLD OCCUPATION.

Having had years of experience in the restaurant business I know whereof I speak, that the Arcade will serve

Better Meals than any House in Town.

Millenery Opening !

MRS. G. W. STEWART

Of San Francisco.

Will open on Tuesday next, November 9, in

Brown's Hotel Block, Fourth St.,

A LARGE ASSORTMENT OF MILLENERY GOODS.

September 10, 1881

STAGE ROBBERY.

The Bisbee Stage Robbed by Three Masked Men.

Thursday night, about 10 o'clock, as the stage was nearing Bisbee, being some four four or five miles this side, in the broken ground, it was stopped by three (some say four) masked men, who, with pistols leveled at the driver and passengers, demanded Wells, Fargo & Co's treasure box. The box was thrown out, when they went through the passengers, getting eight dollars and a gold watch from one and about six hundred dollars from another. From the treasure box they got a fat haul, there being $2,500 in it. The report is that they also went through all the baggage and the mail sacks, but this is rather doubtful.

About 9:30 yesterday morning, two messengers rode into Tombstone with their horses upon a lope, halting in front of Wells, Fargo & Co's office, dismounted and went in. Those seeing the men come in such hot haste, at once surmised something wrong, and in a short time the robbery was the talk of the street. Marshall Williams, agent for W., F. & Co., immediately notified the Sheriff's office, and in a few hours himself, Deputy Sheriff Breakenridge, Wyatt and Morgan Earp were in the saddle or on the way to the place of the robbery, from whence they will take up the trail and do their best to overhaul the robbers. This, we fear, is a hopeless task, as so much valuable time was lost by the messengers riding from Charleston into Tombstone, when they might better have telegraphed and had the whole thing managed in secrecy.

CONTENTION CITY HOUSE.

Contention City - - - - - Arizona.

THE UNDERSIGNED CALLS THE ATTENTION OF THE TRAVELING PUBLIC TO HIS New house in Contention. He flatters himself that he has now filled the bill for long needed accomodations, both in bed and board at Contention City. His beds and bedding ought to please the most fastidious. Good comfortable mattresses with clean sheets, and what goes to make up a bed can be found at the Contention City House. Fire in all bed rooms when required. Attached to the sleeping apartments is a restaurant on first-class principles, and meals can be had at all hours up to 9 o'clock P. M., and for his ability to keep a well provided table he refers to at least one-half of the bachelor boarders of Contention City.

LAUERUER. Proprietor

January 1881

AMERICAN HOTEL, CHARLESTON, A. T.

[illegible], PROPRIETOR.

Nevada Restaurant.

NO. 506 ALLEN STREET, ABOVE SIXTH, TOMBSTONE.

First-Class board at $7.00 per week. Three meal tickets for $1.00. Single meals 37 1/2 cents. Hot Dinners at noon and in the evenings. Unsurpassed by any establishment in Tombstone. Orders for Wedding Cakes and all kinds of ornamental work [illegible].

E. H. JACKSON.
Proprietors.

Arcade Restaurant & Chop House

Allen Street, Vizina Block, Tombstone, A. T.

Miss Nellie Cashman, Proprietress.

LATE OF THE DELMONICO, TUCSON.

Meals at All Hours.

Regular Dinner from 4 to 7 p. m. Open Until 8 p. m.!

DUNBAR BROS.,

LIVERY, FEED AND SALE STABLES,

Fifth Street Between Safford and Fremont

[illegible] OUR STOCK OF SADDLE AND CARRIAGE [illegible] suitable accom[illegible] rates. Good stabling, best of grain and hay and careful attention given to animals left in our care. Boarding by the day, week or month.

THE NEVADA CASH STORE,

ALLEN STREET, NEAR FIFTH.

Miss Nellie Cashman, Proprietress.

Fruit, Provisions and Furnishing Goods

Choice Family Groceries a Specialty,

☞ Fresh Fruits received daily from Los Angeles. A Complete Assortment of Gent's Furnishing Goods and Ladies' and Children's Shoes constantly on hand. Customers and Orders will receive prompt attention.

[illegible] and Examine the Stock.

X. L. N. SALOON,

JOHN W. MEYER, - - Proprietor.

CORNER SIXTH AND ALLEN STREETS.

THISTLE-DEW, GOLD LEAF WHISKY AND FINE CIGARS

DRINKS, 12 1-2 Cents.

Sign of the Balloon.

Pioneer Boot and Shoe Store

The only exclusive Boot and Shoe House in Tombstone, has on hand

A COMPLETE ASSORTMENT OF

BOOTS AND SHOES!

LADIES', MISSES' AND CHILDREN'S

SLIPPERS & SANDALS.

In fact, everything belonging to a First-Class

BOOT AND SHOE STORE.

Fine Ladies' Shoes and Slippers

MADE TO ORDER ON SHORT NOTICE.

Repairing Neatly Done

POSITIVELY ONE PRICE | GIVE US A CALL.

H. KAYSER & CO.

505 ALLEN STREET, Between Fifth and Sixth.

OCCIDENTAL HOTEL

Corner Allen and Fourth Streets, Tombstone.

BROWN'S HOTEL,

CORNER FOURTH AND ALLEN STREET, TOMBSTONE

Conducted on the European Plan.

Single Rooms, $1 per Night. : : : Lodging, 50 cents.

DAILY EPITAPH.
OFFICIAL JOURNAL OF TOMBSTONE.
TUESDAY MORNING, APRIL 19, 1881.

A PRISONER TAKES FRENCH LEAVE.

The Murderer of Schneider at Liberty.

"Johny-Behind-the-Deuce," alias O'Rourke, is Tossed Over the Wall by his Companions and Flies Like a Bird to the Mountains—Over a Sixteen-Foot Wall—Indians in Pursuit—The Sheriff Hopeful, but Other People Not.

"Johny-behind-the-Deuce," or O'Rourke, the party who killed Schneider in Charleston, some months ago and was so near being hanged by a mob both in Charleston and Tombstone, made his escape from the county jail last night about 6 o'clock. The circumstances were as follows: The prisoners had all finished their suppers, and it is customary after this meal to let them out into the jail yard for a few moments preparatory to being locked up for the night. Mr. Roach, the jail-keeper, sat at the door while the prisoners passed out, and Mr. Hersy, another of the guards, stood by to pass them. They all went out into the yard, and a number of them soon passed into the corral behind the jail. When once behind the jail they were out of sight of the two guards. Mr. Hersey says as the last one passed out of the door he, Hersey, brought up the rear with his gun and followed them behind the corral. The escape, he says, must have been made in the interval while he was awaiting the exit of the last prisoner and his walk to the rear of the jail, which he thinks did not occupy twenty seconds.

HOW THE ESCAPE WAS MADE.

How the escape was made is at most conjecture, but it is supposed that his comrades caught O'Rourke and threw him up so that he could grasp the top of the wall. Being active, and having the greatest of all reasons, the saving of his neck, for celerity of movement, he probably slipped over the other side as quick as a flash and dropped easily to the ground, making off as fast as his legs could carry him. Mr. Hersey says his attention was not attracted to the escape of the prisoner until fully five minutes afterwards, when he saw a man bearing the broken shackles of O'Rourke. He then immediately ordered the prisoners to their cells and discovered that O'Rourke was missing. They were locked in and

THE ALARM GIVEN.

Men were put on his track, and skillful Indians employed to trace him, but the near approach of night, the crowd in the vicinity of the depot, where he may have made for, and certainly did make for, if he had any judgment, leaves but little hope of his recapture. Once mixed with the crowd, Indians nor nobody could effect anything in the way of tracking except through a miracle. It would be impossible to conjecture what direction he would take, and any tracking would be the merest moonshine, unless he had some peculiarity about his boots or feet which would give him away.

The most remarkable part of the affair is how they managed, in so short a time, to get him to the top of the wall. The wall about the jail corral is about 16 feet high, and the men must have been both athletic and quick in their movements. Aftr he was once on the wall it was easy enough to drop to the soft earth in the next corral, and the second wall being very low presented no obstacle to his progress. We refrain from comment on the escape at present merely suggesting that where so many desperate men are confined it would have been more prudent to have taken them out for their evening promenade one at a time or to have had a stronger guard. —[Arizona Mining Journal.

April 15, 1882

May 1, 1880

PIONEER STORE

Cor. 5th and Fremont Sts.

JOE HOEFLER, - PROPRIETOR.

— DEALER IN —

Ceneral Merchandise.

MINERS AND RANCHERS

Supplies a Specialty.

AGENT FOR IMPROVED

Agricultural Implements,

And the Celebrated

Turbine Wind-Mills

TENTS, WAGON COVERS,

Buckeye Force-Pumps.

J. O. DUNBAR. J. H. BEHAN.

DEXTER STABLES,

LIVERY, FEED,

—AND—

Sale Stables,

Allen, bet. Third and Fourth Sts.

Stables recently built with modern improvements. All kinds of first-class turnouts, both single and double, provided at short notice. Mountain rigs for prospecting or visiting mines a specialty. Fine saddle horses for ladies and gents always on hand, to hire by the hour, day or week.

Stock Boarded at Most Reasonable Rates

Attentive and experienced hostlers always in attendance.

DUNBAR & BEHAN, Proprietors.

March 16, 1881

Chicken Dinner.
AT
Bayley's Restaurant-To-Day
For 50 Cents.

Lagor—Lager.

Just arrived, a large invoice of John Weiland's celebrated San Francisco Philadelphia Lager Beer. For sale by the glass by our fellow citizen, F. A. Miley, at the Sonoma Wine House, 519 Allen street.

Cachise County Records.

The following is a list of locations and deeds filed for record in the Recorder's Office since our last report.

MINING LOCATIONS.

Yankee Sam, Tombstone, March 12. Geo. Osborne, Ed. Phelan.

Colfax, Tombstone, Jan. 18, J C Baers, M Dinnin, John Gephart.

Hiland Chief, Dragoon Mts., March 14, J R Jordan, Robt. Anderson.

Galore, Chiricahua, Jan. 23, F A Curtiss, John Talt, Chas. L Bassuwell.

Silver Queen, Old Chiricahua, Jan. 29 Niel.

Bruce, Old Chiricahua, Jan. 22, D F Snook, Ed. Alexander.

PONY SALOON.

Allen Street.

As under the former management the saloon will continue to retail nothing but the straight goods, which gave the "Pony" such a well deserved reputation.

T. B. Ripy's Celebrated Anderson County Kentucky (four-year-old sour-mash Bourbon, and

J. M. Atherton's equally celebrated Tea Kettle Rye, of the same age, retailed at 12½ cents.

"LA MARGUESITA,"

The best "Bit Cigar" to be had in the city, a specialty.

T. A. JONES, Proprietor.

Arizona Mail and Stage Comp'y

H. C. WALKER & CO., : J. D. KINNEAR,

PROPRIETORS.

The Lowest Stage Rates!

TOMBSTONE TO BENSON DAILY!

TOMBSTONE TO CHARLESTON DAILY!

TOMBSTONE TO HUACHUCA DAILY!

TOMBSTONE TO HARSHAW DAILY!

TOMBSTONE TO CONTENTION DAILY

Fastest time and Best Stock!

OFFICE WITH WELLS, FARGO & CO.

MARSHALL WILLIAMS, Agent at Tombstone.

Melrose Restaurant,

Fremont Street, Betwten Fourth and Fifth, Tombstone, Arizona,

MRS. M. L. WOODS, Proprïetress.

The Largest and Most Elegantly Furnished Dining Hall in the city.

Careful and Prompt Attention to Guests.

Special Provision Made for Private Dining Parties.

Regular Boarding Eight Dollars a Week: Single Meals, Fifty Cents, 6-tf

July 22, 1880

July 22, 1880

December 3, 1881

Oriental Saloon.

The first Wells-Fargo office in Tombstone.

DAILY EPITAPH

Friday Morning......... Oct. 28, 1881

LOCAL SPLINTERS.

TOMBSTONE M. & M. Co. shipped per Wells, Fargo & Co., yesterday, three bars of bullion, 599 pounds, $8,128.

MORGAN and Virgil Earp were doing as well last evening as could be expected from the nature of their wounds.

THE drill of the Knights of Pythias was unavoidably postponed last evening, but it will come off this evening at 7:30.

THE city was exceedingly quiet yesterday, considering the circumstances. There was but one offender before Judge Wallace's court.

TAX-PAYERS will find an item of interest in our advertising columns. It will be well for all owners of property to scan this column for the next three days.

IN the case of I. Levi vs. B. Baron, in Justice Spicer's court yesterday, for the recovery of $50, cash loaned, judgment for the full amount was given in favor of the complainant.

A LADY who was in the postoffice Wednesday at the time of the shooting, in her fright dropped a pocket-book containing $100 in currency. The finder of the same will be liberally rewarded by leaving the same at this office. The lady upon leaving the postoffice went immediately to her home at the Boston Mill.

THE ORIENTAL is rapidly assuming its old popularity among men of business who meet for recreation and social intercourse. It is conducted with the strictest order and decorum, and the beverages dispensed are of the finest and purest quality. Invalids should read the Oriental "ad." under the head of "New Advertisements."

DAILY EPITAPH

Wednesday Morning..... Feb. 15. 1882

LOCAL SPLINTERS.

A COPY of Acting Governor Gosper's annual report to the secretary of the interior, reached us last evening too late for comment.

ARRANGEMENTS for working the Ingersoll ore have not yet been consummated, but it is supposed that a day or two will decide the question definitely.

THE western mail was late again yesterday. What can the matter be? With the stages runing to Benson we suffered less mail irregularities than now.

A VALVE for the suction was lost from the engine in running to the fire night before last. Any one finding it will confer a favor on the fire laddies by returning it to the engine house.

THE weather thus far this winter reestablishes the faith in the two rainy seasons of southern Arizona. We have, up to date, been favored with an abundance, and at this writing, eleven o'clock p. m., Feb. 14th, the gentle rain is coming down upon the plains, while in the mountains snow is being deposited for an abundant summer supply for the Huachuca Water company.

C. R. BROWN, proprietor of Brown's Hotel, feeling the importance of preparing his premises for the advent of summer, has erected a commodious water closet with the best modern improvements possible until a system of sewerage is adopted for the city. This is a work that all public places should pattern after, and thus ward off this source of contagion. It is an old and wise proverb that says, "An ounce of prevention is worth a pound of cure."

THR Earps and Holliday were taken to Charleston yesterday, escorted by a large party of personal friends, where they appeared in Justice Smith's court. Upon motion of plaintiffs' counsel, Judge Smith remanded them back to Tombsone, where he will appear to-day, at 10 o'clock, to begin the investigation. Briggs Goodrich, Esq., has withdraw from the prosecution, believing, as it is reported, that the present case is mere persecution.

December 30, 1881

BLOODY DEEDS.

A Graphic Picture of Life in Tombstone, Arizona.

How the Cow-Boys Maintain a Reign of Terror—Murders of Daily Occurrence—A Bulldozed Community

From the Kansas City Star.

Mr. J. C. Colyer and wife, accompanied by their two children arrived here this morning over the Santa Fe road, en route from Tombstone, Arizona, to their former home, near Indianapolis. They passed through here last August westward bound, and since that time have seen ten men

DIE WITH THEIR BOOTS ON.

They first located at Socorro, where they were entertained with Indian raids. Mr. Colyer had a lucrative position then as superintendent of a quartz mill, but Mrs. Colyer would not stay on account of the Indian troubles. They then emigrated to Tombstone, where their troubles were made mountainous by the cow-boy raids.

Mrs. Colyer, a bright-eyed, vivacious brunette, about 28 years of age, told an Evening Star reporter a thrilling story of these terrors of Arizona. She says it is impossible to exaggerate the extent to which their lawlessness is carried. The people are all in constant dread of their visits to town, and a citizens' vigilantes committee, several hundred strong, has been organized, which can be called out for active service by a system of signals given with a steam whistle at the hoisting works. The Colyers became intimate with Ike Clanton and Ringo, the

CHIEFS OF THE COW-BOY'S GANG,

during their residence in Tombstone, and through them, met a number of the boys themselves. Mrs. Colyer said of her experiences:

"The cow-boys of that country are most of them polished gentlemen. They are exceedingly polite and courteous. They come to town and stop at the best hotels, and, if in walking through the halls, they meet a lady, they invariably take off their hats and hold them in their hands until they are clear past. Ringo and Clanton are their chiefs. They plan the raids and the others carry them out. Most of them are wealthy, owning the ranches in the surrounding country. I was the witness of one of the bloodiest fights that has taken place in Tombstone for some time. It was October 26th. We were visiting at my brother-in-law's, at Boston Mill. My sister and I drove into the town with the children. All the way in the children kept talking about the cow-boys, and asking what we'd do if we saw any of them. As we drove around the corner, near the post-office, we saw five cow-boys standing in the middle of the road. We stopped at the post-office and my sister went in while I sat in the wagon with the children. We were not fifty yerds from the cow-boys. Presently the chief of police, Virgil Earp, came around the corner, accompanied by his brothers, Wyatt and Morgan Earp, and another man. They were all

ARMED TO THE TEETH.

The sheriff met them and said: 'For God's sake, boys, don't go down there or there'll be war.' The chief of police told him he must go, that it was his duty to disarm the cow-boys who had been making threats against the officers. They approached the cow-boys and told them to hold up their hands. The cow-boys opened fire on them, and you never saw such shooting as followed. Three of the five cow-boys were killed, and two of the officers seriously wounded. One of the cow-boys after he had been shot three times, raised himself on his elbow and shot one of the officers, and fell back dead. Another used his horse as a barricade and shot under his neck. You see their chief had been disarmed that morning by the police and handled pretty roughly, and they were bent on revenge. The cow-boys swore out warrants against the officers, and they had a trial on the

CHARGE OF MURDER,

which lasted three weeks. They were acquitted. The cow-boys are bitter against the Earps and will make trouble yet.

"The Earps own the Oriental saloon and gambling rooms, in which every night from 400 to 500 people congregate. The night before we left the cow-boys had organized a raid on this saloon. Fifteen or twenty cow-boys heavily armed were in the saloon. Just on the edge of town were about thirty more, and others were scattered around town ready to jump into the fight at the signal. A fire broke out and so rustled them that they gave it up for that time. You see we became intimately acquainted with a gentleman who boarded at the same hotel that we did, and who is in sympathy with the cow-boys, and acquainted with all their plans. He told us about this raid being in contemplation, and said that this was the second time they had been all prepared to make a raid, and were thwarted by a fire breaking out and calling all the people out on the streets. He said: You are going away, and I don't mind telling you this."

Editor's Note:

"Mrs. Colyer was an eyewitness who knew none of the gunfight participants, yet she places a gun in Tom McLaury's hand. She also states that, when the Earp party told the 'Cowboys' to hold up their hands, they opened fire on the Earps."

MASSACRE.

Epitaph, January 7, 1882.

By our Tucson dispatch it will be seen that the Indian massacre in Sonora was much more serious than our informants knew of at the time they left Cumpas. It seems there were fourteen men, six women, and four children killed, making twenty-four in all.

We call upon Congress to investigate the late Indian outbreak, and if it can fix the responsibility upon anyone in particular, to award suitable condemnation to the act.

(Epitaph, Jan. 25, 1882)

PROCLAMATION

To the citizens of the city of Tombstone: I am informed by his Honor, William H. Stilwell, Judge of the District Court of the First Judicial District, Cochise county, that Wyatt S. Earp, who left the city yesterday with a posse, was intrusted with warrants for the arrest of divers persons charged with criminal offenses. I request the public within the city to abstain from any interference with the execution of said warrants.

Dated January 24, 1882.

JOHN CARR, Mayor

ANOTHER ASSASSINATION.

Epitaph, 1882.

Tucson, March 21. — This morning at daybreak the trackman at the S. P. found the body of Frank Stillwell, riddled with bullets alongside the R. R. tracks. The shooting is thought to have been done by some of the party of four who accompanied the Earps here to see the body of Morgan Earp off on the night train.

RINGO INDICTED.

January 28, 1882.

The following persons were arraigned in indictment and time for pleading set as follows:

John Ringo, robbery, Tuesday, twelve noon.

Chas. Ewing, robbery, Monday morning, nine o'clock.

Lewis McGinness, grand larceny, Monday morning, nine o'clock.

George Lewis, grand larceny, Monday morning, nine o'clock.

John Bottles, grand larceny, Monday morning, nine o'clock.

In the case of Corneilson, charged with grand larceny, the district attorney moved that a nolle prosequi be entered, which was granted, and the defendent was ordered to be set at liberty.

In the case of John D. Maguire, a nolle prosequi was entered, which was granted, the appeal dismissed and the defendent set at liberty.

Contention vs. Head Center case was then resumed, Mr. Lewis speaking for the plaintiff and Mr. Messick for the defense.

Blaze Extinguished At Coffee Saloon

(Epitaph, Jan. 28, 1882)

A slight blaze broke out last evening about nine o'clock in front of the New York Coffee saloon, on Fourth Street. The lamp in the transparent sign on the outer edge of the sidewalk flared up so as to set the sign on fire; the blaze communicated to the cloth awning and looked for a moment like an incipient conflagration. W. A. Cuddy and other firemen were promptly on the spot, and, climbing the posts, tore off the awning, and put out the fire.

APACHE CHIEF.

Is Reported Killed By Mexicans.

Epitaph, January 7, 1882.

The following special dispatch was sent from Santa Fe, N. M., to the St. Louis Globe Democrat, on Friday, December 30, and if true, is a matter for general rejoicing. The dispatch says:

News has been received from Chihuahua which should be hailed in New Mexico with firing cannon and ringing of bells, Nana, with the sole remnant of his murdering band of Apaches, has been captured and his sub-chiefs executed by the Mexicans. The news, a rumor of which reached us some days ago, comes directly from Presidio Del Norte in Chihuahua, where the scene took place. The Indians, forty in number, led by Nana, came into the Mexican village opposite Presidio and told some of the prominent men there that they had no intention of troubling them. They said all they wished was to trade with Mexico and fight with the Americans. The Mexicans made an agreement to meet them at their camp. The Mexicans went out to the Indians' camp but not to make a treaty of peace. On the contrary, they took the entire band prisoners with the exception of a few men who were out hunting. Then picking out Nana and his chiefs, they led the doomed men aside and drew up the other Indians in line to witness the execution. A firing party of thirty men were then detailed opposite the Indians who were to die, who had been placed with their backs toward their executioners and looking their friends in the face. At his own request, Nana gave the word which sent him and his companions into eternity, and his own vitality was such as to require three more bullets in addition to the two which first pierced his breast, to kill him.

The bodies being buried, the remainder of the Indians were sent, under a strong guard, into the interior of Chihuahua where the women and children were parceled out among the population to work as slaves, and the men were sent on to the City of Chuhuahua, where they will be compelled to work in the mines for the remainder of their lives.

FAST TIME.

A Chinaman's cart pulled by a burro flew down Allen street last night, accompanied by the Chinaman, and the family washing of several citizens. The people along the route yelled themselves hoarse, and the frightened animal renewed his efforts at each shout to increase his speed.

At the corner of fourth street he took to the sidewalk and collided with the awning posts of Patton's old harness shop. Two of them were carried away and the awning toppled over to the sidewalk. The burro and its load went on without any apparent damage, and circled around to Fly's photograph gallery, where it brought up all in good order. A few shirts, collars and undergarments were all that was missing from the load. The Chinaman sat as stolid as a statue on the rear end of his vehicle without showing any signs of emotion over his rapid transit.

Papago Cash Store,

324 Fremont St.. Tombstone

STAPLE and FANCY GROCERIES, Choices Brands of Kentucky Whisky, and grain of al kinds kept constantly on hand and sold at lowes prices.

☞ A ull line of Assayers' Supplies constan on hand.

FRANK B. AUSTIN Proprietor.

CORONER'S JURY.

Report Delayed By The "Ten-Per-Cent Sheriff."

January 22, 1882.

The report of the Coroner's jury on the body of J. Gardner reflects anything but credit upon the sheriff of Cochise county. On the eleventh instant, Gardner died in the county hospital from gunshot wounds inflicted in a railroad camp on the Babarcomari, and on the thirteenth instant, a coroner's jury was convened on the body. It appearing that the case was an aggravated one, that the deceased had been deliberately pierced with four shots, and that the crime had been committed in the presence of a number of witnesses, the jury adjourned until yesterday in order to obtain witnesses and on the sixteenth subpoenas were placed in the hands of the sheriff for one Dan Lehay and another man known as Tex Johnson, two rival saloon keepers. Persuant to adjournment, of eight days, a coroner's jury met yesterday, and are forced through the

CRIMINAL NEGLIGENCE

of a ten-per-cent sheriff, to submit to the public the report to be found in our local columns. It is stench to our new and promising county that the ends of justice are thus thwarted by an officer who has an ample corps of deputies, who could, at least, make a return. The Tucson papers of the twentieth contain accounts of the killing of a Mexican and American on two successive nights and in this dereliction of duty a new impetus will probably be given to the satanic work in the iron-tie camp, but then, Cochise should be content, for do we not have the inestimable privilege of paying one hundred twenty thousand dollars taxation as well as ten per cent thereon? And should not a lightning calculator whose time and figures of the early days of Yavapai are unequaled in estimation of apportionment of representation to be a sufficient boon? Our blessings are many and we should rejoice.

$75 Reward Offered

(Tombstone Epitaph)
(Jan. 28, 1882)

The sum of $50 will be paid for the arrest and conviction of the man who mutilated my day book by tearing out the last two leaves in said book, and the further sum of $25, will be paid for the arrest and conviction of the thief who stole a ledger from my office, together with the return of said book.

C. R. Brown,
Proprietor, Brown's Hotel

TOO MUCH ADO.

Epitaph, 1882.

A great deal of stress is laid upon a barrel of whiskey having exploded in a nearby town recently killing two men. Of course the same kind of whiskey will be drawn from the same kind of barrels for years to come. The quality of said article has not improved a bit in Tombstone since a barrel of it exploded several years ago and set fire to the building in which it was harbored, and caused the destruction of the entire business portion of this city.

KID'S SQUAW SEEKS SAFETY.

(From the Tombstone Epitaph)

The squaw of the notorious Apache Kid has within the past week returned to the San Carlos reservation and asked the protection of the Government. She has been with her notorious chief in all his raids in recent years. Several murders which have been attributed to unknown parties, are now learned to have been the work of the Kid. Her return to the reservation is proof positive of the desperate condition of the renegades. They are practically without food, and she admits she was unable to undergo further hardships of the winter. It will be remembered she has been seen with the band several times within the past few months, and has always participated in their savage deviltries. The band have last been seen in the vicinity of the Dragoons. The squaw is being held under arrest at the reservation.

FIGHT.

Squaws Fight Over Buck.

Epitaph, 1882.

Two squaws had a lively fight yesterday on Fremont Street near Second Street. They discarded their bright colored wrappers, which they usually wear across their shoulders, tied their hair firmly in a loop, so as to obtain a good hold, and with cool deliberation and no back talk placed the right hand in each other's hair and commenced pulling with a gentle swaying movement, which rapidly grew faster; meanwhile the left hands were actively engaged in scratching and punching. A large number of bucks and squaws silently but interestedly viewed the fight. The combatants fought fiercely fully three quarters of an hour without a word, groan or expression of any kind, not ceasing for a moment the hair pulling exercise, until an officer came forward and separated them. The squaws appeared but little hurt, and their black eyes were flashing hatred as they went their own ways.

DEADLY BULLET.

Morgan Earp Shot Down And Killed.

Epitaph, 1882.

At ten-fifty o'clock last night, while engaged in playing billiards in Campbell and Hatch's Billiard Parlor on Allen Street, Morgan Earp was shot through the body by unknown assassins. At the time he was shot he was playing a game of billiards with Bob Hatch, and was standing with his back to the glass door in the rear of the room. He was moved into a card room, where in a few moments he breathed his last surrounded by his brothers Wyatt, Virgil, James and Warren.

CORONER'S INQUEST.

Territory of Arizona, County of Cochise, ss: I hereby certify that the following and annexed papers contain a transcript of the testimony submitted to a jury of inquest empanneled by me as Coroner of Cochise County, A.T., in the Town of Tombstone, A.T., on March 19, 1882, to inquire into when, where and by what means one Morgan S. Earp came to his death, and that the finds of said jury was that death was caused from the effect of a gunshot or pistol wound on the night of March 17, 1882, by Peter Spence, Frank Stillwell, one John Doe Freeze and and Indian called Charlie, and another Indian, name unknown.

H.M. Mathews, Coroner
Cochise County, A.T.

CORONER'S JURY VERDICT

We, the undersigned, a jury empanneled by the Coroner of Cochise County, Territory of Arizona, to inquire whose body is that submitted to our inspection, when, whom, and by what means he came to his death, after viewing the body and having such testimony as has been brought before us, find that his name was Morgan S. Earp, age 29 years, a native of Iowa, and that he came to his death in the City of Tombstone on the 18th day of March, 1882, in the saloon of Campbell and Hatch, in said town, by reason of a gunshot or pistol wound inflictedat the hands of Pete Spence, Frank Stillwell, a party by the name of Freis, and two Indian half-breeds, one whose name is Charlie, but the name of the other was not ascertained.

Signed, J.B. McGowan, Wm. Bourland, Thomas R. Sorin, E.D. Leigh, W.H. Ream, Robert Upton and P. L. Seamans.

Editor's Note:

**"The killers were:
Pete Spencer (not Spence),
Frank Stilwell,
John Doe Freis (not Freeze)
'and an Indian called
Charlie, and another
Indian, name unknown'
(actually Florentino Cruz)."**

1882

ELITE RESTAURANT.

Mush and Milk	.10
Oat Meal and Milk	.10
Cracked Wheat	.10
Hot Rolls	.5
Dry Toast	.5
Mississippi Corn Bread	.5
Corn Batter Cakes	.5
Buckwheat Cakes	.5
Milk Toast	.10
Tea or Coffee	.5

COOKED TO ORDER.

Porterhouse Steak	.25
Sirloin Steak	.20
Rib Steak	.20
Beefsteak	.15
Mutton Chop	.15
Sausage	.15
Fried Bacon	.15
Brains, in batter	.15
Beefsteak, Spanish	.15
Lamb Cutlet Breaded	.15
Fried Ham	.15
Pork Chop	.15

COOKED TO ORDER.

Veal Cutlet Breaded	.15
Liver and Bacon	.15

EGGS.

Ham and Eggs	.20
Ham and three Eggs	.25
Two Fried Eggs	.15
Three Fried Eggs	.20
Omelette, two Eggs	.15
Omelette three Eggs	.20
Scrambled, two Eggs	.15
Scrambled, three Eggs	.20

DINNER BILL OF FARE.

SOUP.

....

FISH.

....

ENTREES.

....

....

ROASTS

Beef.......... Mutton.......... Veal.......... Pork..........

VEGETABLES.

....

PIE AND PUDDING.

....

COMMERCIAL PRINT, 211 FIFTH ST.

April 15, 1882

EXTRA JUDICIAL.

Sheriff Law Superceding Judicial Law in Arizona.

"Crowners" law is a never-ending subject for mirth on the part of those who understand the first rudiments of judicial law, and at the rate the sheriff of Cochise county is going on sheriff law will soon be as great a subject of ridicule. Since the important event of a warrant for the arrest of the Earp party having been placed in his hands by Sheriff Paul, of Pima county, and the walking away of the parties from under the very nose of the sheriff he imagines that every man who is not a personal enemy of the Earps, who happens to leave town in a direction towards where they were last seen, is going to their succor and support, and he at once exerts himself to intercept the person who is so unfortunate as to incur his suspicion. Yesterday afternoon Louis Cooley left town on the Contention stage, on business for Wells, Fargo & Co., going to Benson, where he met J. J. Valentine, Esq., general superintendent of the company, who forwarded him in their own car to Willcox, where he was to complete his business. Much to Mr. Cooley's surprise, upon arriving at Willcox, he was met by Sheriff Behan in person, who demanded his unconditional surrender. Mr. Cooley asked to see the warrant for his arrest, but the sheriff failed to produce one.

There was no resistance—no array of Winchesters or revolvers pointed at the executive officer of the county by Lou—so he was sadly turned over to the custody of the Willcox deputy, with instructions not to allow him to hold intercourse with any one until he was safely landed in Tombstone. Upon arrival in Tombstone Mr. Cooly employed Hon. Wm. Herring as counsel, and went before Justice Wells Spicer and demanded a hearing. Here, upon the demand of Mr. Herring, the warrant was first produced, which was as follows:

Territory of Arizona, } ss
County of Cochise, }

To the sheriff, constable, marshal, or policeman in this territory. Complaint upon oath having been this day made before me, a justice of the peace in and for the above county, by John H. Behan, that the offense of aiding and abetting the Earps and party has been committed, and accusing Louis Cooley thereof. You are therefore commanded by the Territory of Arizona forthwith to arrest the above named Louis Cooley and bring him before the nearest and most accessible magistrate within this county. Given under my hand this 14th day of April, A. D. 1882.

A. E. FAY, Justice of the Peace for said County.

The warrant was a great source of surprise not to say merriment, to all the parties concerned—the court, attorney and prisoner. It will be seen that the charge is most formidable, no less in fact than "aiding and abetting the Earps and party" of — what? That's the question the court had to wrestle with. Judge Spicer, after mature consideration came to the conclusion that the charge did not come within his jurisdiction, therefore, discharged the prisoner. Any man with a grain of common sense will see that the arrest and detention of American citizens upon such frivolous charges puts every man at the mercy of an officer who has any animosity or ill-will towards him. In order to set a wholesome example to the public officers a suit for damages will be forthwith brought against the sheriff, and it will be prosecuted to the end of the law that such an example may be set that peaceable and lawabiding citizens will not henceforth be arrested and detained when on their own or other peoples legitimate business.

Tombstone Epitaph
May 27, 1882

TOMBSTONE BURNS.

THE FIRE.

Tombstone Devastation.

THE FIRE KING REAPS A HARVEST.

Scenes and Incidents of the Great Conflagration.

THE LOSSES.

INDIVIDUAL SUFFERERS.

Re-building Commences.

Full Particulars of the Fire.

Once again has the fiery demon of destruction spread his baleful wings over the fateful town of Tombstone, and once again within a year has the bonanza camp been visited by the fiery scourge. Yesterday morning the bright sun rose over as happy and prosperous a camp as any on the Pacific Coast. Ere the God of day sank behind the western hills a scene of desolation and destruction met the eye in every direction. The blackened walls and smoking ruins of what were once handsome and beautiful buildings is all that remains of what was the very heart of Tombstone. The business portion of the town has been destroyed and many a man and woman who yesterday were in affluent circumstances find themselves today reduced to poverty. The baleful fates which seem to hover over us have once more thrown a deadly blight on our progress and prosperity. But despite the frowns of Fortune, the bonanza city will rise Phoenix-like from its ashes and in a few short weeks what are now smoldering ruins will be built up and ready for business.

Below we give a succinct account of the great fire. No pen can describe the scenes and incidents of the fearful conflagration. The fiery flames rose high in the heavens while dense volumes of smoke obscured the light of day and made Tombstone look like a hell on earth. The shrieks of women, and the imprecations of men, the mad rushing of vehicles, and the indescribable confusion, was a scene long to be remembered. The Epitaph Office had close exertions of our gallant fire department, and the untiring exertions of our gallant printer boys, we are enabled to present to our readers this morning a full account of

THE FIRE

which started in a water closet in the rear of the Tivoli saloon on Allen street. It soon communicated with the framework of the "garden" in the rear of the saloon. The wood being dry, it ignited and burned with the rapidity of cotton. Numerous shanties surrounded the burning pile. Closets, kitchens, store-rooms on the rear, with the wood trimmings on the adobe walls in front, the flames were easily fed. The sumptuous apartments of the Tombstone club in the Grand Hotel building were among the first to kiss the flames; the general building of the Grand Hotel was next embraced in the fiery arm; the wooden staircases on the outside of the building in the rear fell

AN EASY VICTIM.

Next the window frames were taken in and the flames communicated to the interior, and carpets, floors, furniture, etc., fed the fiery elements. An Epitaph reporter immediately after the alarm of the fire, and before the department was yet on the ground, climbed to the top of the adobe building in the rear of the Grand Hotel. A glance was sufficient to convince that the fire would be of enormous extent. All the surroundings were particularly adapted to flame food. In less than fifteen minutes the entire space between Fourth and Fifth streets and

Allen and Toughnut was one steaming, smoking, blazing mess of desolation and ruin. The firemen, than whom no braver body of men or more worthy of thanks exist, turned their attention to the herculean task of saving the north side of the street. But it was impossible.

THE FIREMEN

fronted the flames until most of them were scorched and finally doggedly retreated to keep up their contest in another quarter. The flames spread rapidly. Soon the Occidental saloon was enveloped, the Alhambra soon followed, and the mad sea of vicious fire spread on each side of the Cosmopolitan Hotel on the West, a seething mass of flames. Brown's hotel followed suit and the fire ere many minutes had the Fourth street gun store safely in its arms. Here a scene was presented magnificent in its

LURID FIERCE GRANDEUR.

A large quantity of powder was stored in the cellars, and a number of cartridges and other explosive material were in the store. Here, as soon as the flames were communicated to the combustibles, a wild scene presented itself. The loud bursting of cartridges, the bursting of powder added to the shouting of men and timid screams of women made the air horrible with their resounding echoes. But

THE HEART OF TOMBSTONE

was doomed. None but visionary enthusiasts hoped that anything but the straggling suburbs could be saved. But the hope beats high in the human breast, and the gallant firemen, aided by the police, under Chief Neagie, and a number of deputies under Sheriff Behan, struggled manfully to stem the storm. The wind was not blowing an extraordinary gale, and only the fiery elements had to be fought. The flames reached Fremont and rapidly spread across the entire distance between 4th and 5th streets. At the corner of Fifth and Allen a noble struggle took place. The fiery elements with guant, hungry arms thirsted to cross the street and

CAPTURE THE ORIENTAL.

Here the firemen got in their best work. It was a pitched battle. The weak water and the impetuous onset of the flames made it almost certain that the latter would conquer: But Blackburn rallied his gallant little fire company, a steady stream was poured on and the gaudy destroyer was beaten. Joyce, who suffered so heavily in the former fire came off in this instance with moderate damage. His loss will be about a couple of thousand dollars. All the liquors he had on hand he distributed to the gallant defenders of the city and his house is much gutted up with the water strewn, the porch torn down and most of his glassware either broken, lost or destroyed. But the

FLAMES SWEPT ONWARD.

Fourth street was crossed, the clothing house of Levinthall on the corner of Fourth and Allen was enveloped. The Nugget office was reached and quickly swept from the face of the earth. The other buildings on the same block were quickly swept away. It reached Fremont on that side, but thanks to the combined efforts of firemen, deputy sheriffs, police and citizens, the fire was conquered. The backbone of the fell destroyer was broken and the west end of the block bounded by Third street was saved. The postoffice building went. Schieffelin Hall, the Gird building and the Epitaph were in momentary danger. The Epitaph staff rallied like gallant sailors on a well-be-loved ship, removed the material promptly, and rallied valiantly with buckets to save the building. Their efforts were successful and the Epitaph still holds forth to disseminate the daily news of the world, defend the right and condemn the wrong.

THE LOSSES

are considerable, and will foot up perhaps five hundred thousand dollars, with a probable insurance of half that amount. There are several severely wounded by falling timbers, walls or scorches, but only one death. The unfortunate victim is unknown. His charred remains were found in the rear of the Cosmopolitan hotel after the flames had subsided.

July 6, 1882

COLD BLOODED MURDER.

An Efficient Officer Killed by a Mexican Desperado.

Our citizens were startled yesterday morning by the announcement that Deputy Sheriff Phillips had been killed while attempting the arrest of a disorderly character. At first the rumor was discredited by many, but an investigation revealed that it was only too well founded, and that one of the most dastardly and unjustifia- murders that ever stained the criminal annals of the city had been committed. The facts elicited by the EPITAPH reporter are as follows: About 7 o'clock in the morning a Mexican whose name was subsequently learned to be Filomino Orante entered the saloon of Moses & Mehan, corner Fifth and Fremont streets, and called for a drink. He was evidently partially intoxicated, and soon drew a revolver, which he flourished in a threatening manner. The barkeeper, James Hennessey, remonstrated with the Mexican, and endeavored to have him put up the weapon, but without avail, the latter being evidently in a dangerous humor. Hennessy then dispatched a messenger for an officer, fearing violence from the swarthy desperado. The messenger started in the direction of the Oriental corner, where he chanced to meet Phillips, who was en route to the sheriff's office, to attend to his official duties. Phillips immediately proceeded to the scene of the disturbance, and Hennessy explained the situation of affairs to him, telling him that the Mexican, who had meanwhile stepped out, was armed and evidently desperate, and that he should be careful in approaching him. Phillips then went outside with the intention of arresting and disarming the Mexican. As the former approached, the latter stepped backward and stumbled, at the same instant drawing his revolver and firing, the bullet, with deadly accuracy, striking the doomed officer in the right shoulder, and passing through the wind-pipe, lodging in the the vitals. Simultaneously with the firing of the murderous shot, Phillips drew his own revolver, and after the deadly missile had accomplished its fateful mission and the death film had dimmed his eyes, fired a shot at his slayer. The shot from the dying man's weapon took effect in the right thigh of the murderous wretch, bringing him to the ground. With marvelous tenacity of life, the mortally wounded officer then turned and retreated into the saloon, the blood gushing in spasmodic jets from his mouth, passing through and out the back door, a distance of some thirty steps, falling dead on the threshold. Officer Harry Solon appeared at this juncture and procuring an express wagon conveyed the Mexican to jail. Dr. Goodfellow dressed his wound later in the day, and found that the bullet had broken the hip bone, passing through the rectum and inflicting a dangerous and propably fatal wound. The doctor stated that if the man was in a more suitable place than the jail the chances of his recovery would be largely augmented. When the facts of the murder became generally known, much excitement prevailed, and muttered imprecations and threats of lynching were freely indulged in. Senor Corella, the Mexican Consul at this place, hearing of the threats of lynching, notified Sheriff Behan, who, as a precautionary measure, placed extra guards at the jail. At a late hour last night more prudent counsel seemed to prevail, and little fear of violence to the prisoner was entertained. While his wounds were being dressed the body of Orante was examined and the scars of four old gunshot wounds discovered. He is a native of Hermosillo, Sonora, and it is stated his purpose here was to avenge the death of his countryman, who some time since wounded Officer Poynton and was summarily killed by Chief Neagle in the attempt to capture him.

A post mortem examination of the murdered man, by Dr. Goodfellow, showed the nature of the wound to be as follows: The bullet entered the upper part of right arm, passed through the pectoral muscles in front of the armpit, entered the chest cavity between first and second ribs; thence passed through the upper lobe of right lung; thence through the transverse part of the arch of the aorta—the main artery of the body—at the same time cutting a small hole in the windpipe: thence through the upper lobe of the left lung, in the left side of which it lodged. Death occurred from hemorrhage into the windpipe and pleural cavities. A coroner's jury was impaneled yesterday afternoon, and after hearing some testimony adjourned until 10 a. m. to-day.

At the regular meeting of Rescue Hook and Ladder Company last night a committee was appointed to report resolutions of sympathy at the untimely death of Mr. Phillips, who was an honored member of the company. The same committee was also instructed to take charge of the remains, pending the arrival of deceased's brother.

The murdered man was a native of New York, and twenty-six years of age. He had been a resident of Tombstone about one year, and during the term of the District Court last fall acted as Deputy Clerk, winning golden opinions from Bench and Bar by his gentlemanly deportment and careful attention to business. He was temporarily employed by Sheriff Behan about four months ago, and his efficiency was so apparent that he was permanently retained as a deputy. He was a young man of most exemplary habits and good principles. He was utterly devoid of fear in the discharge of his duty, although most quiet and unassuming in his manner. In short he was a true friend, an upright citizen and an honest and capable official.

The sad news was telegraphed to Ike Phillips, a brother of the deceased, at San Francisco, yesterday, and the following reply was received: "Will leave to-morrow. Have the body embalmed." The deceased has three brothers living in California, and a brother and sister reside in New York.

DEATH OF JOHN RINGO.

His Body Found in Morse's Canyon—Probable Suicide.

Sunday evening intelligence reached this city of the finding of the dead body of John Ringo near the mouth of Morse's canyon in the Chiricahua mountains on Friday afternoon. There was few men in Cochise county, or Southeastern Arizona better known. He was recognized by friends and foes, as a recklessly brave man, who would go any distance, or undergo any hardship to serve a friend or punish an enemy. While undoubtedly reckless, he was far from being a desperado, and we know of no murder being laid to his charge. Friends and foes are unanimous in the opinion that he was a strictly honorable man in all his dealings, and that his word was as good as his bond. Many people who were intimately acquainted with him in life, have serious doubts that he took his own life, while an equally large number say that he frequently threatened to commit suicide, and that event was expected at any time. The circumstances of the case hardly leave any room for doubt as to his self destruction. He was about 200 feet from water, and was acquainted with every inch of the country, so that it was almost impossible for him to lose himself. He was found in the midst of a clump of oaks, springing from the same stem, but diverging outward so as to leave an open space in the centre. On top of the main stem and between the spreading boughs, was a large stone, and on this pedestal he was found sitting, with his body leaning backward and resting against a tree. He was found by a man named John Yost, who was acquainted with him for years, both in this Territory and Texas. Yost is working for Sorgum Smith, and was employed hauling wood. He was driving a team along the road, and noticed a man in the midst of the clumb of trees, apparently asleep. He passed on without further investigation, but on looking back, saw his dog smelling of the man's face and snorting. This excited curiosity, and he stopped the team, alighted, and proceeded to investigate. He found the lifeless body of John Ringo, with a hole large enough to admit two fingers about half way between the right eye and ear, and a hole correspondingly large on top of his head, doubtless the outlet of the fatal bullet. The revolver was firmly clenched in his hand, which is almost conclusive evidence that death was instantaneous. His rifle rested against a tree and one of his cartridge belts was turned upside down. Yost immediately gave the alarm, and in about fifteen minutes eleven men were on the spot. The subjoined statement was made by the eye witnesses to Coroner Matthews:

TURKEY OR MORSE'S MILL CREEK.

Statement for the information of the Coroner and Sheriff of Cochise county, Arizona: There was found by the undersigned, John Yoast, the body of a man in a clump of oak trees, about twenty yards north from the road leading to Morse's mill, and about a quarter of a mile west of the house of B. F. Smith. The undersigned viewed the body and found it in a sitting posture, facing west, the head inclined to the right. There was a bullet hole on the top of the head on the left side. There is, apparently, a part of the scalp gone, including a small portion of the forehead and part of the hair. This looks as if cut out by a knife. These are the only marks of violence visible on the body. Several of the undersigned identify the body as that of John Ringo, well known in Tombstone. He was dressed in light hat, blue shirt, vest, pants and drawers. On his feet were a pair of hose and an undershirt torn up so as to protect his feet. He had evidently traveled but a short distance in this foot gear. His revolver he grasped in his right hand, his rifle resting against the [illegible] ridge belts, the belt for revolver cartridges being buckled on upside down. The undernoted property was found with him and on his person; 1 Colt's revolver, calibre 45, No. 222, containing five cartridges; 1 Winchester rifle octagon barrel, calibre 45, model 1876, No. 21,896, containing a cartridge in the breech and ten in the magazine; 1 cartridge belt, containing 9 rifle cartridges; 1 cartridge belt, containing 2 revolver cartridges; 1 silver watch of American Watch company, No. 9339, with silver chain attached; two dollars and sixty cents ($2 60) in money; 6 pistol cartridges in pocket; 5 shirt studs: 1 small pocket knife; 1 tobacco pipe; 1 comb; 1 block matches; 1 small piece tobacco. There is also a portion of a letter from Messrs. Hereford & Zabriskie, attorneys-at-law, Tucson, to the deceased, John Ringo. The above property is left in the possession of Frederick Ward, teamster between Morse's mill and Tombstone.

The body of deceased was buried close to where it was found.

When found deceased had been dead about twenty-four hours. Thomas White, John Blake, John W. Bradfield, B. F. Smith, A. E. Lewis, A. S. Neighbors, James Morgan, Robert Bolter, Frank McKenney, W. J. Dowell, J. C. McGray, John Yoast, Fred Ward.

From Fred Ward, who arrived in the city on Sunday evening, an EPITAPH reporter learned that the general impression prevailing among people in the Chiricahuas is that his horse wandered off somewhere, and he started off on foot to search for him; that his boots began to hurt him, and he pulled them off and made moccasins of his undershirt. He could not have been suffering for water, as he was within 200 feet of it, and not more than 700 feet from Smith's house. Mrs. Morse and Mrs. Young passed by where he was lying Thursday afternoon, but supposed it was some man asleep, and took no further notice of him. The inmates of Smith's house heard a shot about three o'clock Thursday evening, and it is more than likely that that is the time the rash deed was done. He was on an extended jamboree the last time he was in this city, and only left here ten days ago. He had dinner at Dial's in the South Pass of the Dragoons one week ago last Sunday, and went from there to Galeyville, where he kept on drinking heavily. We have not heard of his whereabouts after leaving Galeyville, but it is more than likely that he went to Morse's canyon. He was subject to frequent fits of melancholy and had an abnormal fear of being killed. Two weeks ago last Sunday in conversing with the writer he said he was as certain of being killed, as he was of being living then. He said he might run along for a couple of years more, and may not last two days. He was born in Texas and is very respectably connected. He removed to San Jose, California, when about sixteen years old, and Col. Coleman Younger, one of the leading citizens of that town is his grandfather. Ringo was a second cousin to the famous Younger brothers now in the Minnesota penitentiary, for their partnership with the James boys. He has three sisters in San Jose, of whom he was passionately fond. He was about thirty-eight years old, though looking much younger, and was a fine specimen of physical manhood. Many friends will mourn him, and many others will take secret delight in learning of his death.

CAUTION—All persons are hereby cautioned against negotiating with jumpers, Clark, Gray & Co., or any other parties but the undersigned, for the purchase of lots 20 and 21, in block 2, as we claim the same by right of purchase, prior location, occupation and improvements thereon. - H. & T. B. COLLINS.

Tombstone, January 5, 1881.

NOTICE.

All persons indebted to Tribolet Bros., proprietors of the Eagle Market, are requested to settle up prior to March 21, after which date outstanding accounts will be placed in the hands of a lawyer. Persons having accounts against the firm are requested to call and present the same.

TRIBOLET BROS.

Cautioned.

ALL PERSONS ARE HEREBY CAUTIONED not to purchase or negotiate for that certain mine known as the Fanny A., as the same is claimed and located by the undersigned.

R. B. CLARK,
R. C. McCEFFREY.

J. W. STWART. JAMES MURPHY

Editor's Note:

"Ringo was born in Indiana (not Texas). Cole Younger was not his grandfather, in fact he was no blood relation at all. Younger was married to Ringo's aunt. Therefore he was not related to the Younger brothers either. He <u>should</u> look younger than thirty-eight years of age, as he was only thirty-two."

DAILY EPITAPH

Wednesday Morning, July 19..........1882.

Sandy Bob's Stage Line.

Office, Well's Fargo & Company's building. Stages leave Tombstone for Contention at 5 a. m. to connect with the eastern-bound train and at 1:00 p. m. to connect with the western bound train. Accommodation stage for Contention will leave every day at 7:30 o'clock a.m. and 2:30 p. m., city time.

Opposition Line.

N. Smith's Opposition Stage Line leaves Tombstone every day at 8 a. m. and 1:30 p. m., and connects with the morning and evening trains at Contention. Fare, **$1.00.**

Mails.

Eastern Mail—including all points east of Benson—closes 9 p. m.

Western Mail—including all points west of Benson—closes 11:30 a m.

Money Order business closes 3 p. m.

Register business closes 3:30 p. m.

No Money Order or Register business transacted after office hours.

Bird Cage OPERA HOUSE.

BILLY HUTCHINSON - - Proprietor.
NEAL PRICE, Director of Amusem'ts.

THIS EVENING
And Until Further Notice.

FIRST APPEARANCE OF
MISS IRENE OSBORNE,
The Charming Balladist in Concerted Selections.

Messrs. Mulligan and Cohan,
The Famous Reel, Jig and Clog Dancers. The Kings of Irish Comedy.

OUR PETITE STAR,
MISS ANNIE DUNCAN.
THE TOMBSTONE NIGHTINGALE.

MR. HARRY K. MORTON,
Comedian and End Man in his Great Specialty. the Dublin Dancing Master.

OUR SERIO-COMIC QUEEN,
Miss LOTTIE HUTCHINSON,
In her Selections of the Latest Gems.

THE EVER POPULAR
MISS CORA STANLEY,
Vocalist and Dancer.

MR. NEAL PRICE.
Author and Vocalist, in his original Budget of Songs of the Day.

General Admission, 25 cents.
Boxes According to Location.

LOOK OUT FOR MULDOONS PICNIC
For cast see small bills. jy16 tf

PEACOCK & DOHERTY.

House, Sign and Carriage PAINTERS.

316 ALLEN STREET, Next to Dexter Stables.

All work done with the utmost dispatch. Good work or no pay. 316 Allen, below 4th.

John P. Rafferty,

OF RAFFERTY & Co.,

—Can be found at—

510 ALLEN STREET,

WITH A STOCK OF FINE CIGARS AND Liquors. Wolesale and Retail. m30tf

REMOVAL.

Robt. G. Westerman,

Formerly of 415 Fremont Street, has removed to corner First and Safford. Any order for

FORGING AND SHEET-IRON

Work will

Be Promptly Done

By leaving same at the Tombstone Foundry. m 31

LEVAN HOUSE!

Furnished and Unfurnished

ROOMS!

533 AND 535 ALLEN STREET
jun20 tf Upstairs.

Can Can Chop House,

HAS

RE-OPENED ON ALLEN ST.,

NEXT DOOR TO ALHAMBRA SALOON,

Where the Proprietors would be happy to meet

WEDNESDAY MORNING, JULY 19, 1882.

SOCIETY NOTICES.

Solomon Lodge U. D., F. and A. M.
The officers and members of the above named Lodge are hereby notified to attend a called meeting thereof this (Wednesday) evening at 7:30 o'clock for work in the second degree. All sojourning brethren in good standing are cordially invited to attend. By order of the W. M.
M. SUART, Secretary.

Estray.

CAME TO MY STABLE, A HORSE branded **SW** on left hip, also branded on left shoulder **W**. Any one owning such a horse can have the same by paying costs and proving property.
L. LARRIEN, French Restaurant, Contention.
jy18 14t

Maud S. Saloon,

J. DOLING, Proprietor.

Has Re-opened !

At the Old Stand, on Allen Street, between Fourth and Fifth.

FINEST BRANDS OF WINES, LIQUORS AND CIGARS.
jy19 tf

FOR CORONER.

I hereby announce myself as a Candidate for the office of

Coroner of Cochise County,

Subject to the nomination of the Republican County Convention.

H. M. Matthews.
jy19 tf

A Mistake.

FOR SEVERAL DAYS PAST I HAVE HAD a notice in the EPITAPH warning all porsons against purchasing the Cochise Mine, situated in Arispe Mining District, Sonora, Mexico. The notice was predicated upon an error. Joe Califero & Co. are the owners of the mine, and have an absolute right to dispose of it.
jy19 1t SALVADOR PIGNATURA.

Removal !

THE GRAND CENTRAL RESTAURANT,

Has Removed from Sixth Street

TO THE LE VAN BUILDING,

ALLEN STREET.

Where they would be glad to meet their old patrons.

MRS. DORNDON, Proprietress.
jy18 3t

MISCELLANEOUS.

JAMES H. TOOLE. CHARLES HUDSON.

HUDSON & CO.,

SUCCESSORS TO

SAFFORD, HUDSON & CO

BANKERS.
TOMBSTONE AND TUCSON.
ARIZONA.

DRAW BILLS OF EXCHANGE
And Make
TELEGRAPHIC TRANSFERS OF MONEY
On the Principal Points in
EUROPE AND THE UNITED STATES.

Receive deposits, purchase or make advances on Territorial and County bonds and warrants, approved commercial paper, etc., etc., and transact
A GENERAL BANKING BUSINESS.
Deposits of Bullion made with us or shipped to Anglo Californian Bank, San Francisco, for our account, can be checked against immediately.

Correspondents:
NEW YORK............J. & W. SELIGMAN & Co
SAN FRANCISCO.ANGLO CALIFORNIA BANK L'D
LOS ANGELES.....LOS ANGELES COUNTY BANK.
ST. LOUIS............BANK OF COMMERCE.
CHICAGO........MERCHANTS S. & T. COMPANY.
BOSTON..............MASSACHUSETTS NATIONAL BANK
PHILADELPHIA....CENTRAL N[illegible]A BANK

Jordan's Lunch Stand,

BENSON, A. T.

HAVING OPENED a FIRST CLASS LUNCH STAND at Bob Stewart's, I solicit a share of the public patronage generally.

MEALS AT ALL HOURS.

The best viands the markets affords will be furnished my guests. When visiting Benson, come in, see me and be convinced.

Single Meals, 50c.; 3 Meal Tickets for $1.00 jy tf

GRAND OPENING ! !
—OF—

SPANGENBERG'S

GUN STORE,

214 FIFTH STREET,

Guns, Pistols, Ammunition, Etc.

AT BEDROCK PRICES.

G. F. Spangenberg.

4jl tf

SCHIEFFLIN HALL

WHITEMAN & HOWE, LEASEES.

3 - NIGHTS - 3

COMMENCING

Thursday, December 4

Mr. Otto H. Krause presents the versatile actor

JACK O. TAYLOR,

SUPPORTED BY THE

KRAUSE-TAYLOR BIG CO

Thursday Night—A True Kentuckian.
Friday Night—Monte Cristo.
Saturday Night—A Gay Deceiver.

Special Scenery and Effects. High class Singing and Dancing Specialties. Prices: Reserved seats $1.00. General Admission: Adults, 75 cents; Children, 50 cents. Reserved seats now on sale at Tombstone Pharmacy.

Cock Pit Saloon,

Allen St., between 6th and 7th.

Best of Wines, Liquors & Cigars.

Cocking Main Every Sunday.

Fair Play in the Pit and the Best Cock Wins.

D. P. WALCH, MANAGER.

jy9 tf

July 19, 1882

A. J. RITTER.

City Undertaker,

—A Full Supply of—

Metallic Caskets for Shipping

KEPT ON HAND.

METALLIC CASKETS, WOOD CASKETS and Coffins, and a good supply of Metallic Burial Cases kept constantly in stock.

THE FINEST HEARSE

In the Territory is connected with this establishment.

my22

RUSS HOUSE,

Corner Toughnut and Fifth.

Cochise County Bank,

TOMBSTONE, ARIZONA.

—DIRECTORS:—

P. W. SMITH, B. M. JACOBS,
L. M. JACOBS, E. B. GAGE,
H. SOLOMON.

[Organized March 18, 1882.]

We offer to the citizens of Tombstone the amplest facilities for the transaction of business, buy and sell exchange on all the principal cities of the United States and Europe, receive deposits payable by check at sight, make collections at lowest current rates, and effect loans on approved security.

P. W. SMITH, Prest.
SOLOMON, Cashier. E. B. GAGE, Vice-

Saddle Horses For Sale.

THE EX RANGERS' OUTFIT, CONSISTing of eleven Horses and two Mules, with Saddles, Rifles, Scabbards, etc., are offered for sale. These horses will stand hard service, are in good condition, and will be sold cheap.

Apply to

G. E. MAGEE,

At Frank Walker's Corral, corner Ninth and Allen Streets, Tombstone.

jy15 tf

LOUIS TAUER,

FORMERLY OF FREMONT ST.,

—HAS—

Opened His Barber Shop,

On Allen, between 6th and 7th Sts.,

Where he will be glad to see his old customers, and is desirous of gaining new ones. Popular prices.

jy10 1m

July 19, 1882

MR. AND MRS. CAMPBELL

....OF THE....

NEW ORLEANS RESTAURANT,

Although burnt out, with no insurance, have once more opened up at

THEIR OLD STAND,

—ON—

Fourth Street, Between Allen and Fremont,

Where they will be glad to see their old and new friends. jl4 tf

July 19, 1882

ANDY'S

CLUB SALOON,

A. ROBINSON.

—IMPORTED—

Wines, Liquors & Cigars.

The same old brands of Cigars, and the best in town for one bit.

IMPORTED

SCOTCH WHISKY

In Judge Spicer's old office.

July 19, 1882

B. C. QUIGLEY,

305 FOURTH ST.,

Notary Public,

CONVEYANCER & GENERAL SOLICITOR. Deeds, Mortgages, Bonds, Contracts, etc., neatly and carefully drawn, money loaned.

HOUSES BOUGHT, SOLD and RENTED.

Collections promptly made, Insurance Solicitor, and general dealer in stocks and securities. j6tf

TALE OF A SHIRT.

January 30, 1892.

Dr. D. S. Chamberlain, who is stopping at the Palace, was a visitor to Tombstone in eighteen seventy-nine. He tells the story of a man being shot down in the street, and the anxiety of his friends to give him a decent burial. They hunted high and low for a white shirt to dress up the remains in, but there was not one in town with the exception of a clean one which the Doctor had in his valise, and which he had been saving to put on when he went "inside." He could not withstand the appeals, however, for a white shirt, and gave it up without a murmur. The last he saw of his boiled shirt it was on the dead body of John Hicks, the murdered man, as he was stretched out in a rough pine box.

December 3, 1881

W. E. MURRAY. M. B. CLAPP

CLAPP & MURRAY,

GENERAL

INSURANCE AGENCY

508 Allen Street.

COMBINED ASSETS

of Companies represented,

$75,000,000!

GUNSMITH. 1880

G. F. Spangenberg,

PIONEER

GUNSMITH and MACHINIST,

Dealer in all kinds of

Guns, Pistols, Sewing Machine Needles, Oils and Attachments, Etc., Etc.

CARTRIDGES AND AMMUNITION

OF EVERY DESCRIPTION.

In Tin Shop, Fourth Street, near Post Office.

REPAIRER OF GUNS, PISTOLS, LOCKS and all kinds of sewing machines, key-fitting. ☞ Lock-box POST OFFICE keys furnished promptly. Apply at Post Office.

N. B.—All kinds of Patterns and Models a specialty. All work warranted.

July 23, 1882

Removal!

THE GRAND CENTRAL
RESTAURANT.

Has Removed from Sixth Street

TO THE LE VAN BUILDING.

ALLEN STREET.

Where they would be glad to meet their old patrons.

MRS. BOURDON, Proprietress.

jy18 3t

Cock Pit Saloon,

Allen St., between 6th and 7th.

Best of Wines, Liquors & Cigars.

Cocking Main Every Sunday.

Fair Play in the Pit and the Best Cock Wins.

D. P. WALCH, MANAGER.

jy8 tf

A. J. RITTER.

City Undertaker,

—A Full Supply of—

Metallic Caskets for Shipping

KEPT ON HAND.

METALLIC CASKETS, WOOD CASKETS and Coffins, and a good supply of Metallic Burial Cases kept constantly in stock.

THE FINEST HEARSE

In the Territory is connected with this establishment. my22

RUSS HOUSE,

Corner Toughnut and Fifth.

HAS BEEN

COMPLETELY RENOVATED

SINCE THE FIRE,

And now has the finest and coolest rooms in Tombstone.

The Table is furnished with all the Market affords.

J. PASCHOLY,

jy13 tf PROPRIETOR.

I hereby announce myself as a Candidate for election to the office of

Judge of the Probate Court of the County of Cochise.

Subject to the action of the Democratic county convention.

James Reilly. jy20

FOR DISTRICT ATTORNEY.

Marcus A. Smith.

Subject to the nomination of the Democratic convention. jy22

H. G. HOWE,

Civil Engineer

—AND—

U. S. Deputy Mineral Surveyor.

MINING EXCHANGE BUILDING,

TOMBSTONE, A. T.

Topographical Maps of Mining properties neatly executed at short notice. Careful reports made upon Mining Properties.

☞ The Best of References Given.

Bird Cage

OPERA HOUSE.

BILLY HUTCHINSON - - Proprietor.
NEAL PRICE, Director of Amusem'ts.

THIS EVENING

And Until Further Notice.

FIRST APPEARANCE OF

MISS IRENE OSBORNE,

The Charming Balladist in Concerted Selections.

Messrs. Mulligan and Cohan,

The Famous Reel, Jig and Clog Dancers. The Kings of Irish Comedy.

OUR PETITE STAR,

MISS ANNIE DUNCAN,

THE TOMBSTONE NIGHTINGALE.

MR. HARRY K. MORTON,

Comedian and End Man in his Great Specialty, the Dublin Dancing Master.

OUR SERIO-COMIC QUEEN,

Miss LOTTIE HUTCHINSON,

In her Selections of the Latest Gems.

THE EVER POPULAR

MISS CORA STANLEY,

Vocalist and Dancer.

MR NEAL PRICE,

Author and Vocalist, in his original Budget of Songs of the Day.

General Admission, 25 cents
Boxes According to Location.

LOOK OUT FOR MULDOON'S PICNIC

For cast see small bills. jy16 tf

CRYSTAL PALACE SALOON !

FORMERLY GOLDEN EAGLE BREWERY.

Ben Wehrfritz, - - Proprietor.

FINEST WINES, LIQUORS & CIGARS.

Fredericksburg Beer Always on Tap, Ice Cold.

First Class Caterers and Courteous Attention.

SEE THE FOUNTAIN !

July 23, 1882

JULY 23, 1882.

The Crystal Palace.

The Crystal Palace Saloon, on the Allen and Fifth streets, was opened last night, and it is no slight to any other establishment to say that it is the finest saloon in the Territory. It is owned by Ben Wherfritz, and he has spared neither labor or money in beautifying and adorning it. A fountain is placed in the middle of the floor, from which spouts forth streams of pure water. The walls are tastefully painted and decorated, and everything arranged with infinite taste. From a platform at the rear end of the saloon a piano, presided over by Mrs. Lincoln, sends forth strains of music, and gambling tables are arranged on each side. This magnificent structure was erected by the well known contractors Messrs. Bruce and Jones and it is as creditable a piece of work as could be performed in any city in the United States. Mr. Bruce paid particular attention to the wood work, and a glance at the counter, and carved door frames will show how thoroughly he understands his business. Mr. Wherfritz will conduct the Crystal Palace as a first-class saloon, and nothing but the best of liquors, wines or beer will ever be dealt over his counter.

LEVAN HOUSE !

Furnished and Unfurnished

ROOMS!

533 AND 535 ALLEN STREET

Jun20 tf Upstairs.

MISCELLANEOUS.

JAMES H. TOOLE. CHARLES HUDSON.

HUDSON & CO.,

SUCCESSORS TO

SAFFORD, HUDSON & CO

BANKERS.

TOMBSTONE AND TUCSON.

ARIZONA.

DRAW BILLS OF EXCHANGE

And Make

TELEGRAPHIC TRANSFERS OF MONEY

On the Principal Points in

EUROPE AND THE UNITED STATES.

Receive deposits, purchase or make advances on Territorial and County bonds and warrants, approved commercial paper, etc., etc., and transact

A GENERAL BANKING BUSINESS.

Deposits of Bullion made with us or shipped to Anglo Californian Bank, San Francisco, for our account, can be checked against immediately.

Correspondents:

NEW YORK........J. & W. SELIGMAN & CO.
SAN FRANCISCO.ANGLO CALIFORNIA BANK L'D
LOS ANGELES....LOS ANGELES COUNTY BANK.
ST. LOUIS............BANK OF COMMERCE.
CHICAGO........MERCHANTS S. & T. COMPANY.
BOSTON..............MASSACHUSETTS NATIONAL BANK
PHILADELPHIA....CENTRAL NA[illegible] BANK

Saddle Horses For Sale.

THE EX RANGERS' OUTFIT, CONSISTing of eleven Horses and two Mules, with Saddles, Rifles, Scabbards, etc., are offered for sale. These horses will stand hard service, are in good condition, and will be sold cheap.

Apply to

G. E. MAGEE,

At Frank Walker's Corral, corner Ninth and Allen Streets, Tombstone. jy15 tf

Daily Tombstone,
Monday, Jan. 4th, 1886

March 17, 1904.

Five shots were fired on Allen street Saturday evening as a result of a dispute between James Parks, a gambler, and Deputy McDonald over the payment of gambling license. Parks fired three shots and McDonald two, neither of which took effect, as a careful search of the morgue failed to find bodies of any of the dead. That some innocent pedestrian was not hit by the promiscuous shooting is regarded as marvelous. Deputy McDonald refused to make a charge or prosecute Parks and the latter was released on one thousand dollar bail on a charge of misdemeanor and later paid a fine of one hundred dollars before Justice Wardwell.

DILLON & KENEALY,

—ARE NOW RECEIVING THEIR—

Spring and Summer

—STOCK OF—

DRY GOODS

—AND—

MEN'S UNDERWEAR.

By our Superior Facilities we are enabled to buy in the Cheapest Markets, and have Determined to give the Public the benefit by selling Goods at the

LOWEST PRICES!

The Latest Novelties,

EVERY DEPARTMENT COMPLETE.

FIFTY PIECES OF

Imported Lawns Bought at Auction

We Will Sell at 10c. per Yard—A Desirable Bargain.

DILLON & KENEALY,

Fifth Street, Bet. Allen and Fremont.

July 23, 1882

SAMUEL BLACK,

MERCHANT TAILOR.

NEXT DOOR TO HUDSON & CO.'S BANK.

FIFTH STREET. TOMBSTONE,

Keeps the Largest Assortment of Goods in the Territory. First Class Workmanship and Perfect Fit Guaranteed. Cleaning, Repaing and Binding.

PRICES TO SUIT THE TIMES. 16jy tf

GENERAL BLACKSMITHING,

HORSE-SHOEING AND WAGON-MAKING.

GRAF & SCHOENHOLZER, : : Cor. Third & Fremont Sts.

THE COSMOPOLITAN,

ALLEN STREET, TOMBSTONE, A. T.

Headquarters for All Stage Companies.

C. S. BILICKE, Proprietor.

Carleton's Coffee, Oyster and Chop House,

523 Allen Street.

MEALS AT ALL HOURS AT ANY PRICE.

Every thing First-class. The most comfortable Eating House in the City. San Francisco and Tombstone Daily Papers. Give us a call and we will guarantee perfect satisfaction. LUNCHES PUT UP FOR TRAVELERS.

Mack's Chop House,

411 FREMONT STREET.

Adjoining the Theater Building.

HAVING RECENTLY RETURNED TO Tombstone, I beg leave to inform my numerous friends and former patrons that I have opened at the above place, where it is my intention to furnish the BEST MEAL IN TOWN for 25 CENTS.

J. J. McGRATH.

ICE-CREAM SALOON.

BANNING & SHAW,

Have always on hand the best ice-cream and fresh home-made candies. Ladies and gentlemar please give us a call.

Fourth Street, Above Fremont.

R. CLIFFORD,

—OF THE—

UNION MEAT MARKET.

Would inform the public that he still sells the best of

American Meats

Of every description, Wholesale and retail, at the lowest possible margins to suit the times.

Allen Street, bet., Fifth and Sixth.

April 15, 1882

GRAND HOTEL,

ARCHIE McBRIDE & CO., Proprietors,

ALLEN STREET, TOMBSTONE, A. T.

This Hotel has recently been Refurnished in the Latest Style throughout, and will be found Elegant in All its Appointments. It is conducted on the

European Plan.

Stages and Hacks from Contention City in thirty minutes.

THE BEST APPOINTED HOTEL IN ARIZONA.

July 23, 1882

Thieves About.

Sometime during the early part of Tuesday night an entrance was effected by thieves into the rear room adjoining Danner and Owens' saloon and a quantity of blankets stolen. No clue has been had as yet to the thief or thieves. This is the third or fourth time lately we have heard of depredations of this kind, indicating that the town is being worked by a band of petty larcenists.

Star Chop House.

MRS. MAGGIE McGIVLEY HAVING PURchased this well known and Popular Chop House, will in the future have the tables supplied with

All the Delicacies of the Season.

BOARD, $8.00 PER WEEK.

MAGGIE McGIVLEY,
Proprietress, and successor to Mrs Paddock
jy6 tf

July 23, 1882

MR. AND MRS. CAMPBELL

....OF THE...

NEW ORLEANS RESTAURANT,

Although burnt out, with no insurance, have once more opened up at

THEIR OLD STAND

—ON—

Fourth Street, Between Allen and Fremont.

Where they will be glad to see their old and new friends. jl4 tf

B. C. QUIGLEY,

305 FOURTH ST.

Notary Public,

CONVEYANCER & GENERAL SOLICITOR, Deeds, Mortgages, Bonds, Contracts, etc., neatly and carefully drawn, money loaned.

HOUSES BOUGHT, SOLD and RENTED.

Collections promptly made, Insurance Solicitor, and general dealer in stocks and securities. j6tf

July 23, 1882

OLLOS AND BONES.

Discovery Made by Laborers in the Sonoita Valley—Five Ollos Filled with Human Bones—Ancient Coins Discovered—A Study for Antiquarians.

Gradually but surely a concatenation of evidence is being secured to connect the real and prosaic present with the dim and distant past. Arizona is rich in antiquarian lore, and its history and origin has long been a study for the philosopher and scholar. The esequias of ancient construction, the solidity of which can puzzle competent latter-day engineers; the old ruins of fortresses and churches; the solid habitations of unique build have long been a puzzle to the antiquary. As was hinted at the beginning of this article, the net-work of obscurity that connected these monuments, with a past age, is gradually being rent asunder, and the full beams of a nineteenth century sun is exposing the history and origin to the gaze of the present generation. A few days ago a party of railroad laborers, while excavating on the line of the Arizona and N. M. R. R., in the Sonoita valley, about six miles below Crittenden station, found five ollas imbedded several feet under the surface in a lava formation. Two of these ollas were shaped like wash basins, while the others had the common form. All these utensils were filled to the brim with human bones, complete in every instance except the skull. The fingers, toes, joints, etc., were distinct in every instance. The ollas were cast in the same pattern, and molded of the same material as the common every day articles we are so familiar with. In addition, however, the ollas resurrected in the Sonoita valley were decorated on the inside, with crude symbols and quaint hieroglyphics. In one of them were discovered two Spanish coins, bearing the date 1534. These were set on the top of the bones. Around the rim of the ollas, and expanding over the tops were some very fine roots. One of the vessels was completely covered with this substance. While the skulls were not entire all the broken fragments of that part of the human frame were easily determined. At that part of the valley a lava formation extends for about thirty miles, and the appearances indicate that the lava had run down and enveloped the ollas, with their contents. Not less than three feet of this eruptive substance was found on top of the crude pottery. The bones looked as if they had been burned, and it is a question for naturalists and antiquarians to determine if they were scorched by the burning lava, or whether the body of which they had once been a part was subjected to partial cremation, after the flight of the spirit of life.

Tradition and church histories inform us that a Spanish Padre penetrated the wilds of Arizona about the year 1543, and converted tribes of the wandering nomads to his form of worship. Under his auspices churches and religious houses were built, the chase abandoned for agricultural pursuits, savagery partially surrendered and the Light of the Gospel established. It is more than likely that this missionary taught the unsophisticated savages the rudiments of agricultural science, learned them the theory of irrigation and under his watchful care had the esequias that are still a wonder and admiration built. It is probable that the Spanish coins were introduced by the missionaries, and if so, it is proof positive that Christianity had dawned in Arizona as early as 1550. The ruins in the vicinity of Phœnix and Casa Grande are certainly of ancient date, and almost an assured fact that the Indians did not build them without some preception. We call upon Colonel Poston to take this matter under consideration, and inform us as soon as possible how these bones found their way into the ollas, and how the ollas in turn crawled under the lava.

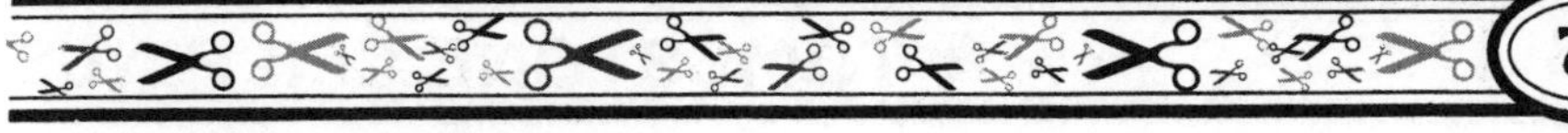

July 23, 1882

ANNOUNCEMENT OF CANDIDATES.

Candidate for Sheriff

OF COCHISE COUNTY,

G. W. BUFORD,

Subejct to nomination by the Democratic party.

Independent of all Rings, Cliques or Combinations. jy8tf

To the

Democrats of Cochise County!

I HEREBY ANNOUNCE MYSELF AS A

Candidate for Sheriff

Before the Democratic Convention. As there are said to be about as many candidates for this office as there are voters I may have a show in the race. I am, gentlemen, very respectfully, your obedient servant.

M. McDOWELL,

jy11 tf Charleston, A. T.

LARKIN W. CARR

IS A CANDIDATE FOR THE OFFICE

Of Sheriff of Cochise County,

At the ensuing election, subject to nomination by the Democratic County Convention. jl2 tf

For Sheriff.

DAVID NEAGLE.

At the request of many friends, I hereby announce myself as an

Independent Candidate

FOR SHERIFF OF COCHISE CO.

To remain in the field until the close of the polls on election day. jy16

For Treasurer.

I hereby announce myself as a Candidate for

Treasurer of Cochise County,

H. SOLOMON,

(Subject to nomination by the Democratic Convention.) jy16

For District Attorney of Cochise County,

George H. Howard,

(Subject to the action of the Democratic Convention.) jy16

For County Recorder

I hereby announce myself as a Candidate for

County Recorder of Cochise Co.

(Subject to nomination by the Democratic Convention.) jy13

A. T. JONES.

FOR CORONER.

I hereby announce myself as a Candidate for the office of

Coroner of Cochise County,

Subject to the nomination of the Republican County Convention.

H. M. Matthews.

jy19tf

July 23, 1882

MISCELLANEOUS.

W. A. EASTMAN,

CARPENTER, CONTRACTOR

—AND—

BUILDER.

Only $150 lost, but still ready for business.

John P. Rafferty,

OF RAFFERTY & Co.

—Can be found at—

510 ALLEN STREET,

WITH A STOCK OF FINE CIGARS AND Liquors. Wolesale and Retail. m30tf

REMOVAL.

Robt. G. Westerman,

Formerly of 415 Fremont Street, has removed to corner First and Safford. Any order for

FORGING AND SHEET-IRON

Work will

Be Promptly Done

By leaving same at the Tombstone Foundry. m 31

Daily Tombstone September 11, 1886

The Fountain.

The Fountain Chop House is the cool?? place in the city to take a meal. No smo heat or smell from the kitchen, it being tirely separate from the dining room. fore-quarter beef used. Nothing but choicest cuts, fish, game, oysters, etc ... ate entrance from Toughnut street to- boxes: oct7,

July 23, 1893

Board of Supervisors.

TOMBSTONE, July 22, 1882.

Board met as a Board of Equalization at 11 a. m. Present—Chairman Joyce and Supervisor Vizina. Absent—Supervisor Solomon.

Minutes of the previous meeting read and approved.

On motion, Board adjourned until 4 p. m.

The Board met pursuant to adjournment at 4 p. m.

Board adjourned until Monday 11 a. m. July 24th, 1882.

RICHARD RULE, Clerk of Board.

Friday night some sneak thief entered the house of Tony Kraker, on Seventh, between Safford and Bruce streets, and made a haul of some clothing and blankets. The house is occupied by Mr. Kraker and G. A. B. Berry. A valise containing a suit of clothes and some underclothing was solen from the latter, and the former is minus a coat and a pair of blankets. A lady residing near the house noticed a man unlock the door and enter, but thought he had the permission of the owners, and took no further notice of him. The police are on the watch for the robber, and if he escapes their vigilance he is a good one.

Notice to Settlers on Lots in Tombstone.

The owners of the TOWNSITE TITLE to lots within the original survey of three hundred and twenty (320) acres in Tombstone, desire to say to those who wish to obtain deeds, that the injunction which was sued out against the Townsite owners has now been finally dissolved, and that there is now no suit or other legal obstacle to making deeds.

The Townsite owners have the legal title to the lots. Their title is under the patent of the United States.

They and their predecessors in interest located the Townsite and paid the United States for the lands entered and patented.

The law of the Territory expressly declares that they shall be considered and held to be the occupants, and that statute has been approved by Congress.

The Townsite owners are now prepared to sell lots on reasonable and liberal terms.

Deeds can be obtained for less than it will cost to litigate.

Apply to the undersigned, corner Fremont and Sixth streets.

J. S. CLARK, Agent and Owner.

ASSAYING.

Henry W. Kearsing.

CHEMIST AND ASSAYER,

SPECIAL CARE TAKEN IN ANY TESTS OR ASSAYS THAT MAY BE PRODUCED.

One assay for gold and silver	$1 50	Five assays for gold and silver	$5 00
Two assays for gold and silver	2 00	One copper assay	2 00
Three assays for gold and silver	3 00	Two copper assays	3 00
Four assays for gold and silver	4 00	Three copper assays	4 00

Lead, Tin and Bullion in Proportion.

☞ Special contracts with companies. Assaying taught on reasonable terms.
OFFICE on Fourth Street. Near Post Office.

COMSTOCK

BARBER SHOP,

OPENED ON AUGUST 9TH,

At 509 Allen Street,

A Few Doors Above Fifth.

First-Class Tonsorial Artists.

Are always ready to shave their old patrons and the public.

PEYSER & LIPPERT. Proprietors.

Dancing School!

—IN THE—

CITY HALL,

EVERY TUESDAY AND THURSDAY.

(Afternoon and Evening.)

SOIREE EVERY SATURDAY EVENING

BILLY REED, Proprietor.

BOILER AND STEAM FITTINGS

415 Fremont Street, Tombstone, A.T.

Billiard Parlors.

Next Door to Wells, Fargo's Expres Office, Allen Street.

CAMPBELL & HATCH, Proprietor

24 KILLED BY APACHES
(Epitaph, Jan. 7. 1882)

By our Tucson dispatch it will be seen that the Indian massacre in Sonora was much more serious than our informants knew of at the time they left Cumpas. It seems there were 14 men, six women and four children killed, making 24 in all.

We call upon Congress to investigate the late Indian outbreak, and if it can fix the responsibility upon anyone in particular, to award suitable condemnation to the act.

P. W. SMITH.

General Merchandise and Banker,

Cor. Allen and Fourth Streets, Tombstone.

The Alhambra.

T. H. CORRIGAN, - - Proprietor.

Elegantly re-fitted and just re-opened with the finest stock of **Wines, Liquors** and **Cigars** ever brought to Tombstone.

My stock embraces the famous **O. K., Cutter, Hermitage, Old Government** and **Stonewall** brands. Imported Brandies. My wines and liquors have been especially selected for the Tombstone trade and can not be surpassed for age and bouquet. **Cigars** were made to order and of the choicest Havana tobaccos.

The Old Boys are notified that the Latch String is always on the outside

---

$500 REWARD.

JOHN H. BEHAN, SHERIFF OF COCHISE County, is hereby authorized and directed to offer a reward of five hundred ($500) dollars for the apprehension of the person or persons who murdered M. R. Peel at Charleston, on the 25th day of March, 1882. M. E. JOYCE,
Chairman Board of Supervisors.

$500 REWARD.

JOHN H. BEHAN, SHERIFF OF COCHISE County, is hereby authorized and directed to offer a reward of five hundred ($500) dollars for the apprehension of the person or persons who murdered Patrick McMinimen, on the San Pedro River, in this county, on or about the 1st day of March, A. D. 1882. M. E. JOYCE,
Chairman Board of Supervisors.

Graf & Schoenholzer,

HORSE-SHOEING, WAGON-MAKING

—AND

GENERAL BLACKSMITHING

West End Corral.

FREMONT AND SECOND STS.,

TOMBSTONE, - - ARIZONA

CHAS. N. THOMAS, Proprietor

HORSES AND STOCK BOARDED ON THE most reasonable terms. Horses bought and sold. The best accommodation for horses and mules.

Saddle Horses For Sale.

THE EX RANGERS' OUTFIT, CONSISTing of eleven Horses and two Mules, with Saddles, Rifles, Scabbards, etc., are offered for sale. These horses will stand hard service, are in good condition, and will be sold cheap.
Apply to

G. E. MAGEE,

At Frank Walker's Corral, corner Ninth and Allen Streets, Tombstone. jy15 tf

April 15, 1882

GRAND OPENING

—OF THE MAMMOTH—

FURNITURE & BEDDING ESTABLISHMENT

OF TOMBSTONE

THE UNDERSIGNED BEGS TO INFORM THE PUBLIC THAT HE HAS NOW OPENED the LARGEST FURNITURE HOUSE in the Territory, and has the best selected Eastern-made Furniture ever imported to the Pacific Coast, all solid Black Walnut, Oak, Ash and Maple. I also carry the finest stock of Carpets, consisting of Ingrains, Tapestry, Rockaberry and Brussels Carpets. Also Oil and Cork Cloths of all widths, and an elegant assortment of Chromos, Engravings and Oil Paintings, Window Shades, Cornices, Lambrequins, etc., constantly on hand. Also the celebrated Hoy Patent Sofa Bed, Parlor Sets, Turkish Chairs, Willow-Ware and Baby Carriages. Having made connections with the best and largest Factories in the East, and shipping by the carload, I am able to sell cheaper than any other house in the Territory

Orders from the Country Promptly Attended to and Satisfaction Guaranteed

NOS. 317 319, 321 ALLEN STREET, TOMBSTONE, A. T.

J. LENOIR.

BIRD CAGE
Opera House

BILLY HUTCHINSON - - Proprietor.
NEAL PRICE, Director of Amuse'ints.

GRAND
MASQUERADE
BALL!

Wednesday Evening
July 26, '82.

Two New Eastern Stars
Appearing on this occasion.

The Ball will be Conducted Strictly First-Class.

Dressing Rooms for Ladies. Accommodations for Gentlemen.

Masks Raised at 12 O'Clock.
15 MINUTES NOTCE GIVEN.

ELEGANT! REFINED!!

Don't forget the Day or Date.
WEDNESDAY EVENING JULY 26.

In addition to our New Olio and Finale.

To the Public.

Having purchased the entire interest of Jos. Pascholy in the undertaking business in this city, I will hereafter devote my especial attention to said business Embalming and the preparing of bodies for removal a specialty. Orders fulfilled in any part of the county.

8-2-tf A. J. RITTER.

July 26, 1882

FOR CORONER

I hereby announce myself as a Candidate for the office of

Coroner of Cochise County,

Subject to the nomination of the Republican County Convention.

H. M. Matthews.
jy19tf

For Coroner.

I hereby announce myself as a candidate for the office of

Coroner of Cochise County.

Subject to the action of the Democratic county convention.

Patrick Holland. jy20

I hereby announce myself as a candidate for election to the office of

Judge of the Probate Court of the County of Cochise.

Subject to the action of the Democratic county convention.

James Reilly. jy20

FOR DISTRICT ATTORNEY.

Marcus A. Smith.

Subject to the nomination of the Democratic convention.
jy22

Dr. John Sullivan

DENTIST.

Allen St., Bet. 7th and 8th.

Has engaged the services of DR. W. PERKINS, Dentist—late of New Haven Conn.

Dr. Perkins has had Fifteen Year's experienc in some of the best offices in the East, an comes to this city highly recommended.

DENTISTRY

In all its branches performed in a neat an substantial manner. Our aim shall beto pleas our patients in work and prices

M. NARDINI.

— DEALER IN —

CHOICE FAMILY GROCERIES,

Allen Street Corner of Fifth, Tombstone, A. T.

THE BEST OF FAMILY FLOUR, HAMS, BACON & LARD.

Canned Fruit Six and Seven Cans for $1.00,

French and Italian Wines

Whisky by the Gallon or by the Bottle.

Fine Imported Cigars, at From $30 to $75 per M.

I sell my goods for CASH and can undersell any merchant in Tombstone. Give me a call. Anything that a person desires in the Grocery line is kept in Stock at my Store.

N. NARDINI.

Corner of Sixth and Alen Streets.

SHAFFER & LORD,

Commission Merchants

AND DEALERS IN

GENERAL MERCHANDISE.

Corner Fremont and Fifth Streets.

IRON, STEEL, POWDER AND CHEAP LUMBER, MINING AND MILLING Goods a specialty. Tees, Elbows, Nipples, Bushings, Globe Valves, Check Valves, Service Cocks, Whistles, Packing, Etc. Choice Groceries, Dry Goods, Boots and Shoes, Hats, Liquors and Cigars. Having made special arrangements to secure Goods at the Lowest Figures, we are prepared o supply our customers with Goods at Reduced Rates, and in any quantity. Sugar, Six Pounds for 1.00. Coffee, Four Pounds for $1.00. Tobacco, One Pound for 80 Cents.

New Firm !!

HOOKER & BAUER.

MEAT MARKET.

WHOLESALE AND RETAIL!

At the old stand of A. Bauer, corner of 4th and Fremont Sts., and at C. S. Abott & Co.'s, Allen Street.

Having entered into a general partnership in the Butchering Business, we will supply the BEST OF BEEF from only American Bred Cattle, and defy competition.

H. C. HOOKER. A. BAUER.

OCCIDENTAL TONSORIAL

BARBER PARLORS.

Under Occidental Hotel.

Two First-Class Artists Always in Attendance.

Hair Cutting, Shaving, Shampooing, Artistically done.

CHILDRENS' HAIR NEATLY CUT.

MARKS & WITTIG, Proprietors.

THE FASHION SALOON,

Allen Street, between Third and Fourth

Keeps Constantly on Hand the Celebrated

McBreyer an

Tea Kettle

Whiskey

Also the famous

COSMOPOLITAN CIGARS

Which is Manufactured Especially for Me.

. S. BRADSHAW, Proprietor.

FASHION STABLES

Having purchased the rolling stock and horses [illegible] J. O. Dunbar, also making many additional purchases, I am now prepared to offer to the [illegible] public the

FINEST TURN-OUTS

Ever brought to the Territory, and on Reasonable Terms.

TRANSIENT and BOARDING ANIMALS

Carefully Cared For.

ALLE ST., Bet. 3d and 4th.

A T. JONES, Prop'r.

Pony Saloon,

ALLEN STREET.

HENRY CAMPBELL, Prop.

CHOICE BRANDS OF

Liquors and Cigars.

St Louis Lager Beer, English Ale and Porter on draught.

☞ MIXED DRINKS A SPECIALTY. ☜

JAMES VOGAN

Liquor Dealers,

ALLEN STREET, TOMBSTONE.

Choice Liquors at Wholesale, in packages of Five Gallons or less.

CUTTER AND MILLER WHISKIES

A Specialty.

A Sample Room Attached.

CALL AND SEE!

☞ Agents for the well known house of H. Horton, Tucson.

HOTELS AND RESTAURANTS.

Headquarters Kinnear's Stage Company.

Cosmopolitan Hotel !!

THE LARGEST HOTEL IN THE DISTRICT. Having completed my second story addition, I am enabled to offer the traveling public very superior accommodations.

Table Supplied with Everything the Market Affords.

Thankful to my friends for past patronage, I respectfully solicit a continuance of the same.

C. BILICKE, PROPRIETOR.

The Cochise Hotel

Cor. 4th & Toughnut Sts.

Only First Class Hotel in Tombstone.

LARGE, LOFTY ROOMS

Elegant Parlor for Guests.

Sample Rooms for Commercial Travelers

A. COHN & BROS.

Allen Street Near Fifth.

Imported and Domestic Cigars and Tobaccos.

Pipes, Smokres' Articles and Fancy Notions.

☞ GIVE THEM A CALL ☜ mr7tf

Special Telegram to the Epitaph

The San Carlos Indians Broke Loose and Fighting Near Fort Apache

(Daily Epitaph)
(Sept. 3, 1883)

The following special telegram appeared in the Arizona Daily Star yesterday morning, and there can be no doubt of its truth. This comes as an additional complication to the many ills that this border land is just now suffering from. Fortunately the department commander is a live man and will spare no exertions to bring the renegades under proper subjection again:

ON THE WARPATH

CAMP THOMAS, Sept. 1,—There has been great uneasiness in Apache County for the past two weeks over rumors that the White Mountain Indians near the fort were excited and ready to break out at any time. On the 15th, Gen. Willcox, commanding this department, sent the available troops in the southern territory to assist in quelling any disturbance of the Indians, who were reported to be excited by bad medicine men, who promised to raise the dead warriors and clear out the whites. But the time of these miracles having passed, and no signs of hostilities appearing, the soldiers were sent back to their posts. Gen. Carr, of the sixth cavalry, was at Fort Apache with some scouts and several companies, and there seemed to be no apprehension of danger; but today a courier arrived from the commanding officer there stating that Carr was out to protect the settlers and had been fighting all day on the 30th, losing a number of soldiers. Couriers sent to him had not returned, though 24 hours over due. Gen. Willcox has ordered out all the troops from Fort Grant and Thomas, and they were marching all last night. They have crossed the Gila River and are pushing on rapidly to Carr's relief. Troops from Fort Lowell and the southern posts are already in motion, and Gen. Willcox takes the field to direct in person the movements of his troops.

LATER. — Tiffany, agent at San Carlos reports that Indian runners have come in from the White Mountains with flying rumors of fighting near Fort Apache. One lieutenant and a number of soldiers are said to have been killed in a fight on Cebicu Creek. Owing to the late heavy storms the military telegraph line is down beyond Camp Tomas, and news came from Fort Apache by mounted courier.

OFFICIAL ACCOUNT

The following is official:

To Capt. Haskel, Aid-deCamp, Fort Bowie: Jut and Geronimo went across the river on a pass from the agency to hunt the day after you left, Monday, and are reported peaceable. Natchez was here to see me this morning. He knows of the outbreak, and says he and the other chiefs are friends, and that he will not allow any of his men to participate in the present troubles. He went to the subagency afterwards. Nothing new since my dispatch of this morning. Perrin's and Craig's companies and Bailey's Indian scouts crossed the river en route to Apache and Biddle, with A and F companies, and Lieut. Overton are crossing now.

(signed VIVEN), Commanding.

TOMBSTONE STORE,

R. R. GOODE, PROPRIETOR,

DEALER IN

General Merchandise.

COMPLETE OUTFIT FOR PROSPECTORS.

California Made Boots and Clothing.

The Best Assorted Stock of Family Groceries in Tombstone District.

MARK P. SHAFFER,

Business Manager.

EATON & RICE,

—Dealers in—

DRUGS AND MEDICINES

Toilet Articles, Patent Medicine.

Physicians prescriptions carefully compounded day and night. Store on Allen Street.

Go to

CADWELL & STANFORD'S

To Fill Your Orders.

GENERAL MERCHANDISE; MINers' Supplies a Specialty.

Tombstone & Tucson

STAGE LINE,

LEAVING RAILROAD TERMINUS EVERY day at 8 a. m. Concord Coaches are run on this line. Good meals en route at reasonable rates. Fare, $7, Currency.

All orders should be left at the Stage and Express Office, in Eaton & Rice's Drug Store, Tombstone, where they will receive prompt attention.

Passengers will register and pay fare at the office.

J. D. KINNEAR, Prop.

JOE EATON, Office Agent, Tombstone.

GRAND SOCIAL DANCE

Gage Hall

To-Night, July 23rd

After the Show

Music by the Famous Phoenix Indian School Orchestra

Everybody is Welcome

Admission - - $1.00

M. EDWARDS,

CALIFORNIA VARIETY STORE!

Corner Allen and Fourth Streets, TOMBSTONE.

Wholesale and Retail Dealer in General Merchandise.

KEEPS CONSTANTLY ON HAND A LARGE Stock of all kinds of goods and sells

CHEAP FOR CASH.

COME AND SEE FOR YOURSELF.

J. M. CASTANEDA. - - MANAGER.

THE DRAGOON

SAMPLE ROOMS.

The Best of Wines, Liquors and Cigars kept constantly on hand.

A reasonable share of the Public Patronage Solicited.

P Lynch, Prop.

ELITE SALOON

—AND—

Billiard Parlors.

Allen Street, Above Fourth
(North Side.)

Keeps constantly on hand the finest quality

—of—

Imported Wines, Liquors and Cigars.

FIRST CLASS CLUB ROOM ATTACHED

Long, - - - Prop.

Bonanza Saloon

I. LEVY. Proprietor

COR. FOURTH AND ALLEN STS.

(Opp. P. W. Smith's)

Tombstone, - - - Arizona,

FINEST WINES AND LIQUORS

Always on hand, Wholesale and Retail.

[illegible]

CIGAR STORE

UNION NEWS

DEPOT.

The largest and best assortment of

Books, Toys,
Stationery,
Musical Instruments,
Periodicals,
Magazines, Etc.

Fine Cutlery and Fancy articles of all kinds always on hand.

Allen Street, Grand Hotel Building.

Sol Israel, Prop.

H. K. TWEED,

Dealer in

General Merchandise

Groceries,
Clothing,
Liquors,
Etc., Etc.

Corner of Fourth and Allen streets.

TOMBSTONE, ARIZONA.

Frank C. Earle,

Assay Office

—AND—

CHEMICAL LABORATORY.

SAMPLES BY MAIL

Will receive Prompt and Careful attention.

Special Rates Given to Mining Companies and Tributers

309 Fremont Street, Tombstone.

OCCIDENTAL HOTEL,

Cor. Fourth and Allen Sts,

TOMBSTONE, A. T.

Pascholy & Tribolet, Prop's,

JOS. PASCHOLY, MANAGER.

This Hotel is conducted on the European plan. Open Day and Night.

Rooms New, Clean and Comfortable.

ROOMS FROM 50 CENTS TO $2 PER DAY.

A first class Restaurant is attached to the hotel, and guests have the use of

An Excellent Billiard Parlor and Private Card Rooms.

LYNCH MOB.

They Came From Bisbee With One Purpose; To Lynch Heath.

Justice moved fast following the Bisbee Massacre. On December sixteenth, a posse led by Deputy Sheriff John Hoover captured Sample and Howard near Clifton. Special officer Tucker captured York Kelley at Deming, N. M., and he was soon behind the bars in the county jail at Tombstone.

Deputy Sheriff Daniels trailed Bill Delaney into Mexico. Disregarding international law, he picked Delaney up at Minas Priestas Mine in Sonora and brought him across the line. Big Dan was caught down in the Sierra Madres.

With the exception of John Heath who tried to mislead the posse, all the outlaws were tried before Superior Court Judge D. H. Pinney early in February, 1884. The verdict of the jury was quick—"Guilty of murder as charged." They were sentenced to hang and on March 8 just a little over three months after they had shot up Bisbee, the outlaws met their fates on the gallows erected in the courtyard.

John Heath was tried separately. As he had not actually participated in the massacre, the jury found him guilty of murder in the second degree. His sentence was life at Yuma prison," but the citizenry didn't quite see it that way.

Tombstone had hardly brushed the sleep from its eyes when the grim cavalcade rode through town. A few housewives cooking early breakfast saw them pass. In front of the courthouse they dismounted. Sheriff Ward answered the pounding on the jail door. As he swung it open he looked into the barrels of several six-shooters.

"Hell! I thought it was the Chinaman bringing breakfast," he gasped as he handed over the keys to the cells.

Heath was cool as they led him to a telephone pole west of the courthouse on Toughnut street. As he stood there seemingly unperturbed at the turn of events the grim Bisbee men asked, "Got anything to say before you swing, Heath?"

His only answer was, "Don't fill me full of holes after you swing me."

With steady hands the outlaw took a red bandana from his pocket and tied it over his face. When the noose was slipped around his neck he seemed to sense a certain amateurishness. "Shove it under my ear," came the muffled voice from under the bandana.

The Bisbee Vigilantes slipped out of Tombstone as quietly as they had come. Few local citizens knew what had happened. Miners and merchants going to work saw a dead man hanging from a telephone pole. When they came near to look they read a placard fastened below his feet which read: "John Heath was hanged to this pole by the citizens of Cochise County for participation as a known accessory in the Bisbee Massacre, at 8:20 a.m., February 22, 1884."

Crook May Leave

(Tombstone Democrat, Jan. 9, 1886)

A telegram received Thursday announced that General Crook will shortly be superseded by General Miles. The change will be welcomed by nearly every citizen of southern Arizona. The former has lost the confidence of the people by his repeated failures to put a stop to Indian outrages. It remains to be seen whether General Miles will be any more successful than his predecessor.

Crystal Palace Theatre,

TOMBSTONE, ARIZONA.

B. WEHRFRITZ, Sole Proprietor,

First-Class Performances Nightly.

Wit, Fun and Frolic, but no Vulgarity.

☞The best conducted place of amusement in Arizona Territory.

.Special Performances,

Every Friday evening for Ladies and Children.

Orchestra and Music the best obtainable. First-class artists employed and always in demand. Troupes or artists in order to obtain engagements must correspond or confer with the proprietor direct.

B. WEHRERITZ,

Proprietor Crystal Palace Theatre, cor. Allen and Fifth Sts.

Crystal Palace Saloon,

(CONNECTED WITH THE THEATRE.)

Choicest Brands of Foreign and Domestic

WINES, BRANDIES,

WHISKIES, LIQUORS, ETC., ETC.

Best brands of

Cigars, Cigarettes, Etc., Etc.,

Imported and Domestic, always on hand.

Crystal Palace Gambling Saloon,

Allen street, corner of Fifth.

☞None but Square Games allowed. The before-named three branches of the above establishment are conducted under the direct management of

B. WEHRFRITZ, Proprietor.

PIONEER STABLE,

I. N. PECK, Prop'r.

Near the Occidental Hotel.

TOMBSTONE, ARIZONA.

Le Van House,

[illegible] and [illegible] ALLEN ST.. OPPOSITE WELLS, FARGO & Co's, TOMBSTONE, A. T.

This Hotel is conducted on the European plan. Open night and day. Rooms new, clean and comfortable. Meals 50 cents. Rooms from 50 cts. to $2 per day. Wm. A. LE VAN, Proprietor.

PIONEER SODA WORKS

C. F. RILEY & CO., Proprietors.

Manufacturers of Soda Water, Ginger Ale, Syrups,

GUMS, APOLINARIS, CIDER, SELTZER SIPHON WATER.

TOMBSTONE, - - - ARIZONA.

☞ Orders taken from all parts of the Territory. Satisfaction guaranteed.

Garf & Schoenholzer,

HORSE SHOEING, WAGON MAKING

—AND—

General Blacksmithing,

CORNER THIRD AND FREMONT STS., TOMBSTONE, A. T..

HOLLIDAY, HOLLIDAY, FEARED WAS THE NAME "DOC" HOLLIDAY.

From Georgia he came with a college degree
And a little black bag in his hand,
With eyes cold as ice, any man would think twice
Before saying hello to this man.
Holliday, Holliday, feared was the name "Doc" Holliday.

A dentist by trade, a gambler by choice,
The road that he traveled was rough.
Brought on by strong drink and a thorn in his flesh,
This man was tougher than tough.
Holliday, Holliday, feared was the name "Doc" Holliday.

Thinking he had but a short time to live,
He raised all the hell that he could.
He was not a good man, but evil,
Yet he did all the evil things good.
Holliday, Holliday, feared was the name "Doc" Holliday.

If he had stayed in bed on that October day,
No lines of history would he now fill,
And the Boothill marker might read Wyatt, Virg. and Morgan
Instead of Tom, Frank and Bill.
Holliday, Holliday, feared was the name "Doc" Holliday.

By rights he should have died with his boots on,
But fate had a hand in this play.
Not by hot lead or cold steel did he pass from this earth,
He died in a peaceable way.
Holliday, Holliday, feared was the name "Doc" Holliday.

—K. W. DeBerry.

A young lad having six fingers on each hand and six toes on each foot was an object of much curiosity on Allen Street yesterday.

The Tombstone Epitaph. Feb. 21, 1887

The Prospector and Tombstone Epitaph after they merged.

THE

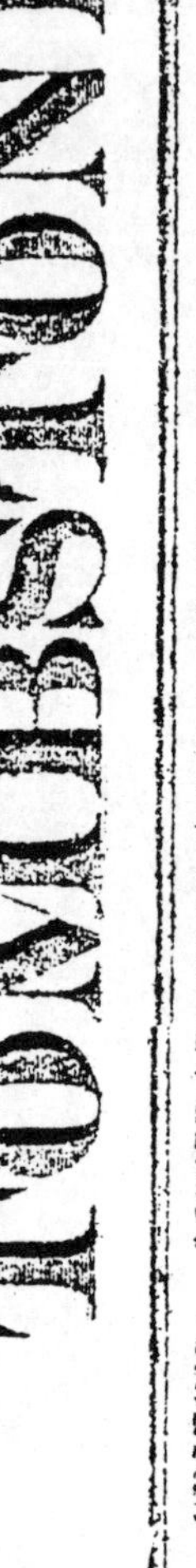
TOMBSTONE.

TOMBSTONE, ARIZONA, MONDAY EVENING, MARCH 30, '85.

THE TOMBSTONE.

The Pioneer Daily of the Camp.

SATURDAY EVENING, - - MARCH [illegible], 1885.

PUBLISHED EVERY EVENING,

(Sunday Excepted)

—BY—

JAMES J. NASH,

Office on Allen Street, north side between Third and Fourth.

Delivered by Carriers for 25 Cents a Week

TOMBSTONE FOUNDRY

AND

MACHINE SHOP

McAllister & McCone, Props.

ALL KINDS OF MILL AND MINING MAchinery, Heavy and Light Castings of Iron and Brass made to order on short notice. Stamps Pans, Settlers, Retorts, Cages, Cars, Skeets, Bailing Tanks, etc., from latest designs. Portable Hoisting Engines, 5-stamp Prospectors' Mills made to order. Screens of all descriptions punched or slotted. Engines indicated and adjusted. Agents for Albany Lubricating compounds, Cylinder, Spindle and Valve Oils. Westinghouse Automatic Engines from 2 to 200 horse power, and all else in the Machine and Foundry line.

James P. McAllister Manager.

Frank C. Earle,

Assay Office

—AND—

CHEMICAL LABORATORY.

SAMPLES BY MAIL

Will receive Prompt and Careful attention.

Special Rates Given to Mining Companies and Tributers

[illegible] Fremont Street, Tombstone.

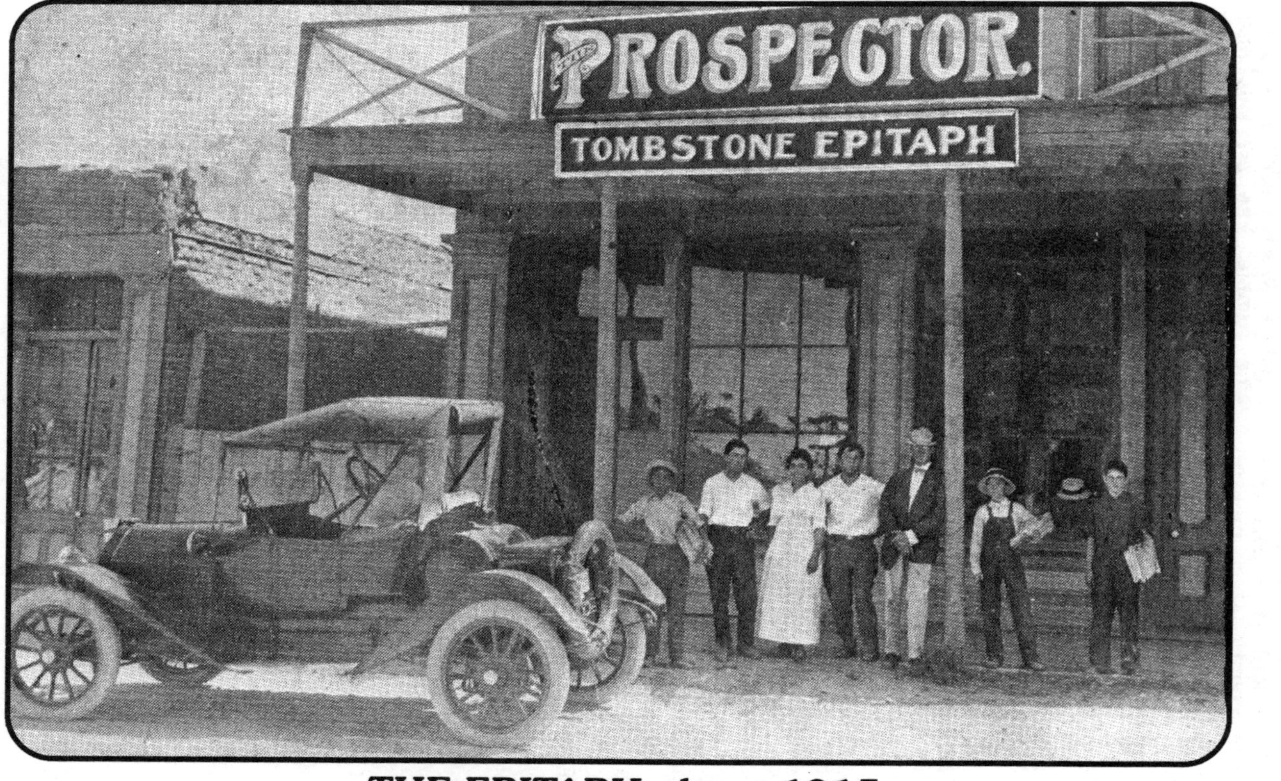

THE EPITAPH about 1915

This photo was made during time the papers were owned by the Giragy family, when the office was still on Freemont Street across from the City Hall. Pictured from left, are: George, Colombus, Mary and Carmel Giragy, Richard Dick, the "Brian Boy", and Orrin Preston.

$500.00

November 17, 1885

By virtue of authority vested in me by the Board of Supervisors of Cochise county at a regular meeting of said board, held on the sixth day of October, eighteen eighty-five, I hereby offer a reward of five hundred dollars for the apprehension, dead or alive, of the renegade Apache Chief Geronimo. And by the same authority I offer a further reward of two hundred fifty dollars for the apprehension, dead or alive, of any one of said Geronimo's band of renegade Indians who have been engaged with him in his murderous raids through Cochise county. Said apprehension to earn the above rewards must be made by some person or persons not in the military service of the United States.

R. S. Hatch
Sheriff
Tombstone, Arizona,
October 6, 1885.

TO INSPECT BOUNDARY.

Epitaph, June 15, 1886.

Surveyor Howe leaves to-day to inspect the new boundary line between this and Pima county. George W. Parsons will accompany him. A private letter from Tucson states that the chairman of the Pima county supervisors has applied to General Miles for a guard to Mr. Howe, and it is believed the general will give him five men.

Virgil Earp writes a letter to Marshal Dodson of Prescott, dated Colton, Cal., saying that he intends to return to Tombstone to live. Extremely doubtful.

August 28, 1887.

A very perceptible earthquake shock was felt in this city at seventeen minutes to twelve o'clock last night. It was preceded by a noticeable rumble, like previous ones. The vibration was from north to south, and lasted about ten seconds.

An Arizona Product.

Dr. G. E. Goodfellow, of Tombstone, one of the leading young physicians of this country, arrived in Phenix yesterday, en route from San Francisco to Tombstone. Dr. Goodfellow furnished the data to the Washington Institute of the recent Sonora earthquakes, and his ideas, theories and scientific analysis of the huge quake, was adopted by Capt. Dutton, of the above institute, as the most thorough and comprehensive that has been furnished for the past twenty-five years. Captain Dutton stands at the head of the scientific world as authority upon such matters, and such a splendid endorsement, coming from such a source, makes us feel proud of our famous young Arizona scientist. Dr. Goodfellow possesses many splendid qualities of both heart and brain. —Phenix Gazette.

TOMBSTONE, A. T.

First-Class in every Respect

CENTRALLY LOCATED.

Rooms Elegantly Furnished. Parlor for Guests.

SAMPLE ROOM FOR COMMERCIAL TRAVELERS.

Daily Tombstone
September 11, 1886

Referring to the above we would say that we will endeavor to give the public the same courteous treatment and fair dealing they have received in the past from Mr. A. J. Ritter.

JOS. PASCHOLY & Co.
Successors to A. . RITTER.
4 29-1w

For the finest pickled pigs feet in the city, go to Martin O'Laughlin's butcher shop, corner Seventh and Fremont streets. 5 7-tf.

HORSE STOLEN

From G. Machin; Slaughter, Alvord Searching.

January 31, 1887.

A Mexican entered the premises of George D. Machin on the corner of Seventh and Fremont streets early this morning and stole a valuable horse belonging to that gentleman. When Mr. Machin discovered that his horse had been stolen he at once notified Sheriff Slaughter who at once took steps to recover the animal. Burt Alvord mounted on a fleet horse and proceeded at once to Fairbank, and about one mile east of that village found the horse, the Mexican either being too closely pursued or the animal was getting tired, consequently the horse and the rider parted. The Mexican thief is well known to the sheriff and also to Machin and a close watch will be kept for the individual. It is presumed he left for Sonora.

GEN. MILES KILLED.

A Bullet From A Government Gun Sends Him To Eternity.

Shot Down At The Head Of Command By Indians.

A special to the Citizen says: Early this morning a courier arrived at the Pine Ridge agency, with the information that a terrible battle was in progress in the Bad Lands. The troops are clearly outnumbered and are in danger of annihilation. THe loss of many lives on both sides is certain. In the first of the fight General Miles rode at the head of his command and before the firing became general, he fell from his horse, shot through the heart and expired. Further particulars are hourly expected.

WITCHCRAFT.

An Idea Probably Taken From A Mast Missionary.

September 24, 1888.

A number of Mohave Indians in San Bernardino county, California, afflicted with what is believed to have been typhoid fever, were beaten with clubs in order to "drive the devil out of their burning bodies" and dragged through the Colorado river "for the purpose of cleansing them of the evil spirit." Yet, curious as it may seem, they died. The Indians, thoroughly mystified by the failure of these effective restoratives, concluded that the tribe was under the spell of a witch, and accordingly burned a young squaw at the stake who was suspected of being a fell and evil-minded sorceress. How this horrible incident will affect the Massachusetts Indian-lovers it is difficult to predict with certainty, particularly as burning women for witchcraft was once a favorite Massachusetts idea.

A Newly Made Bride Seeks Redress At The Hands Of The Court.

October 1, 1888.

Readers of the Epitaph will remember the wedding notice of Sam'l Allen and Mrs. Darrow, which appeared not long since, and now it is the painful duty to chronicle that the honeymoon has been obscured by angry clouds, and the promised conjugal felicity shattered by the shafts of contention and wrath. The casus belli is not known; sufficient is it that she whom Samuel promised to love, cherish and protect, appeared in Justice Easton's court this morning and had a warrant issued for her liege lord's arrest, on the charges of committing an aggravated assault upon her. The trial is set for nine o'clock to-morrow morning.

ON AN EDITORIAL RAMPAGE.

May 6, 1887.

We dislike to discuss family matters in our columns, as everybody knows, but the story that Jeff Tarlton is telling around town about our difficulty last Tuesday night is a lie such as nobody but a dirty coyote would be guilty of. We have heard of him and his gassing at Dan Geehen's saloon. The facts are that we told this red-headed slouch to stop keeping company with our daughter. When we returned home Tuesday night about eleven o'clock we found him just leaving our front porch. There were words, and we admit that we called him a greasy tramp. When he made a pass for us we grabbed him by the whiskers, and when he broke away we kicked him in the small of the back, and the only regret now is that we did not break his backbone. The lie that he tells is that we drew a gun, which he snatched and then ran us in the house. Nobody saw the fracas, and of course he can lie, but John Hapgood, across the way, heard the salute that we gave him as he clawed the gravel down the street. Don't come our way again, Jefferson.

CAN CAN ROBBERY.

Robbed During Night Owner Reports.

Kicker, October 8, 1888.

Early this morning when Mrs. J. Hanninger of the Can Can restaurant opened up for business she discovered that a robbery had been committed during the night and the safe containing $500 in money had been relieved of its contents. Investigation of the robbery develops the fact that whoever was the guilty one, he certainly was well acquainted with the premises and had no trouble whatever in accomplishing his designs.

During Mr. Hanninger's absence at Tucson, serving as U. S. grand juror, Mrs. Hanninger not knowing the combination merely kept the safe on "day combination" a turn of a few notches opening it at any time. The safe was left in this condition making it an easy matter for the intruder, who undoubtedly knew of the circumstances, to open the safe and make away with the money drawer.

Besides, in effecting an entrance through the rear, having first climbed over an adobe wall into the yard, the robber was on friendly terms with the watch dog, a vicious one, for the dog made no noise and was turned out into the street.

April 23, 1894.

The combination of a small boy with an express wagon going one way and a big man going the other resulted in a collision that turned the air sulphurous in the vicinity of Overlock's butcher shop for a few minutes this morning.

A BLOODY TRAGEDY.

George Davis Shoots Pietra Edmunds and Commits Suicide.

Epitaph, April 14, 1888.

Our usually quiet city was thrown into the most intense excitement yesterday by a tragedy such as never before occurred here. About 2 o'clock in the afternoon, passers-by on Third street, near Safford, observed a young man, George Davis by name, running after a young woman named Pietra Edmunds, and firing at her with a six shooter. He fired three shots, one of which took effect in the womwn's shoulder, after which he placed the pistol to his temple, pulled the trigger and the ball went through his brain, causing death in a few minutes.

The cause of the tragedy was jealousy. Young Davis had been paying attention to Miss Edmunds, but day before yesterday, it is stated that they quarreled, and this so preyed upon the young man's mind that his reason, never very strong, became dethroned. He had recently come from Casa Grande, near which place he is said to have some valuable mining claims, and found on his return that he had been replaced in the affections of the young lady.

At the time of the shooting Miss Edmunds was passing by the residence of the unfortunate young man's father, corner of Third and Safford, in company with Fred Stone, when young Davis ran out of the house, revolver in hand, and pointed it at Stone. The young woman screamed and ran across the street towards her own home. This diverted Davis attention from Stone, who ran up town after an officer. In the meantime Davis pursued his former sweetheart to her very door, firing as they ran. Only one bullet took serious effect. It entered the back of the young lady near the shoulder blade, passed through the right lung and out of the breast. At 9 o'clock this morning (Saturday) she was resting easily, and there are strong hopes of her recovery.

George Davis was 21 years old, and was always considered a quiet, honest, industrious boy. His parents are highly respectable people and have the most sincere sympathy of the people of this community. The bereaved mother is now in California. The fond father takes the loss of his oldest son very hard.

The young woman who was the cause of the trouble (perhaps innocently) is about 17 years old and is the daughter of the late Eugene Edmunds (known as "Stockton"), her mother being a Mexican, and also dead. She is quite pretty, and is wroth some property.

An inquest will be held on the body of Davis at 2 o'clock this afternoon at Ritter's undertaking rooms, and the funeral will take place at 2 o'clock tomorrow (Sunday) from the same place.

TOMBSTONE, ARIZONA, APRIL 14, 1888.

TOMBSTONE.

A Youthful History of the Bonanza Mining Camp.

Some time since the Superintendent of Public Instruction offered a prize to the scholar in the public schools of the Territory who would write the best sketch of his or her town, and in response to the request the following was written regarding Tombstone by Rosie Hattich, aged 11 years, daughter of our fellow townsman B. Hattich. It is well worth reproduction:

TOMBSTONE.

Tombstone is a rather funny name. It was so called by a man named Al Schieffelin, who, when he was coming out here wanted a party of men to come with him. They were afraid of the Indians, and told him he would not find his fortune but his tombstone.

Tombstone is located in Cochise county, and is the county seat. The latitude of Tombstone is 31 degrees 43 minutes north. The longitude is 110 degrees 05 minutes west. Tombstone is 10 miles from the San Pedro river. The nearest railroad station, called Fairbanks, is ten miles away.

The altitude of Tombstone is 4,600 feet above the level of the sea. The thermometer ranges from 29 degrees to 103 degrees above zero. The rain comes very irregularly, occuring mostly in July and August. The total for 1887 at Camp Huachuca was nineteen inches. The snow falls about twice a year, lasting from three to four hours, and sometimes, four or five days on the mountains.

The surrounding mountains are the Dragoons on the north-east, the Huachucas on the west, the Mules on the south and the Whetstones on the north-west. The valleys are the Sulphur Spring valley, on the south-east, the San Simon valley on the south-east, the Barbacomari and the San Pedro on the west.

The chief mineral is silver. Others are gold, copper and a small amount of lead.

There are two articles manufactured, as and ice.

The agricultural products are corn, wheat, barley, alfalfa and all kinds of vegetables. Stock raising is carried on in the valleys, where there is plenty of water. The soil is very much like that of California, and if it gets enough water, will yield abundantly.

The principal occupation of the people is mining.

The first settlement was made by Schieffelin at Watervale, because there was no water elsewhere.

There are no Indians in this county, only those who come to buy provisions and sell ollas. These are called Papagos. They are partly civilized, were converted to Christianity by the early Catholic missionaries, and they still cling to that faith. They rendered many valuable services to the whites during the long contest with the Apaches.

There are four churches here, the Episcopal and the Methodist, which are both adobe buildings. The Catholic and the Presbyterian, which are both frame buildings, the Catholic and the Episcopal have towers with bells.

The other public buildings are the Court House, the City Hall, the Skating Rink, Schieffelin Hall and the School House. The last is a frame building, and has two halls and six rooms; 250 pupils attend school.

There are about eight hundred private buildings, mostly constructed of wood and adobe.

The trees are chiefly cottonwoood, umbrella, weeping willow, oak and the ash.

The animals are cows, horses, sheep, pigs and mules. The wild animals are the coyote, the antelope, the squirrel, the rabbit and the gopher.

There are many birds, such as the blue bird, black bird, the mocking bird, the canary, the dove the quail, the hawk, the owl and the crow.

There is a very small amount of fish caught. Mr. Igo has a fish pond where fish are caught, but it is only an artificial pond. Some fish are caught in the San Pedro river.

Some of the reptiles are the hoop snake, rattle-snake, gater-snake, copperhead, lizard, the centipede, tarantula and scor pion

Some of the fruits are cherries, currants and strawberries.

The honor of being the oldest inhabitant of Tombstone lies between Mr. Harwood, Mr. Bauer, and Mr. P. Bahn Warnekros.

The first earthquake that occurred here was on the third day of May, 1887. It did no damage except cracking of adobe walls and frightening of people.

Tombstone is one of the most famous mining towns. Ore was discovered in February, 1877, by A. E. Schieffelin.

The Copper Queen is the chief mine of Bisbee, and the great copper mine of Arizona.

It was discovered in 1877 by Hugh Jones, and relocated by Geo. Warren, Ray ("Kentuck") Elderman and others. They gave an interest to Geo. Anhurtz, for doing the assessment work. In the same year Warren bet his interest in a foot race, and lost it, the winner being G. W. Atkins. In 1880 Jas. Reilly bonded the mine for $28,000 The original founder, Jones, gave it up, as he could see nothing but copper stained rock.

Evidences of civilization still exist at the mouths of the Ramsey and Miller canyons in the way of adobe and stone ruins, which have by the action of time and weather, crumbled and decayed, leaving traces and outlines of streets and large buildings, whose foundations of stone crop out through the crumbled masses. Stone hatchets, pottery, arrow heads of flint, all go to show that these places have been inhabited by some ancient race.

In Cochise Stronghold are to be seen hieroglyphics and characters made by Indians. In the Huachucas are numerous caves, such as the Montezuma, containing stalactites and stalagmites and other interesting and attractive formations. Some of the stalactites being small and in rows, give out clear and distinct notes like a piano when you pass your fingers over them. Some of the stalactites resemble wax works.

The Huachuca mountains are 9,600 feet above the sea level. There is a fort in the Huachuca mountains called Camp Huachuca, in which there are a number of very handsome buildings. The surroundings are also very handsome.

The Huachuca Water company get their water from these mountains. This water has the most force of any brought to Tombstone.

Arizona produced the largest nugget of silver ever found, its weight being 2,700 pounds. In February, 1878, Al Schieffelin and Richard Gird located the Toughnut, Lucky Cuss, Contention and other mines, all in Tombstone, which have since that time, produced many millions of dollars for their owners.

The country in which the mines are situated may be described as a series of rolling hills.

1888

Prospector
May 17, 1903

John Slaughter went through yesterday on his way to Colorado. Mrs. Slaughter came in from the ranch with him and stopped in Tombstone.

May 5, 1888.

John Hill and John Roberts were in town Thursday. They were exceedingly jubilant over the victory of the little roan pony, which succeeded in defeating the best blooded stock that could be brought against him . The race took place in Phenix Saturday last—Hungry John being the loser—distance 500 yards, for a purse of $600. Cochise county is hard to down, when it comes to men, horses or pumpkins.

The assignment of H. K. Tweed has been the one theme that has been of paramount interest in Tombstone business circles this week. He brought a large capital to the Territory and has been one of our most energetic and progressive citizens. His misfortunes have called forth the sympathy of all who are acquainted in the manner in which his losses have been brought about.

It has been practically decided at the war department to assign Major-General Crook to the command of the division of the Missouri with headquarters at Chicago. It is said that Major General Howard, commanding the division of the Pacific, desired to be transferred to the Missouri, but it was found that the interests of the service would be sustained better, by retaining him at San Francisco, and assigning the new Major General to the division of the Missouri.

The supreme court of Mexico has confirmed the sentence of death passed on Colonel Francisco Arvizagas, for having authorized the violation of American territory and an attack on American peace officers at Nogales in March, 1887.

Mrs. John H. Slaughter, accompanied by her daughter Addy and son Willie, will leave soon for San Antonio, Texas, to visit the parents of Sheriff Slaughter.

A. H. Davis, so well known in this city, has secured the position of door-keeper at the Territorial Insane Asylum in Phenix.

Invitations are out for a wedding which is announced to take place about the middle of the month between a young lady who is very popular in Tombstone society and a young business man who is equally popular. The event is to be celebrated in Phenix.

The third day of May just past, is a date long to be remembered in the annals of Southern Arizona. The great earthquake occurred on that day one year ago.

Don't forget the big Sunday dinner at the new Elite Restaurant to-morrow.

Charlie Bartholomew, the efficient police officer, has recently purchased a neat cottage residence on Second street and has removed his family thereto

He's Also a Good Looker.

Fred Dodge made his appearance on the streets yesterday, with the nattiest express rig ever seen in Tombstone.

The wagon was built in San Francisco, and is a poem in its way.

The horse is the handsome dapple gray, formerly owned by A.J. Ritter, and these taken in connection with the fact that Fred himself is away over the average in good looks, makes a combination not often seen.

—The Epitaph, Jan. 15, 1888.

FATAL SHOOTING.

Epitaph, August 29, 1888.

Albuquerque, August 29. — Geo. Lee was shot and killed by Chas. H. Jackson in the street this morning. Lee's sister was married last night to Jackson, who is an ex-convict, and Lee threatened Jackson's life. Meeting the latter in the street to-day, Lee fired several shots at him, none taking effect. Jackson returned the fire, the first shot proving fatal. Jackson was arrested.

Every man needs a wife, because among the many things that go wrong are a number he can't blame on the government.

FOR SUPERVISOR.

I hereby announce myself as a candidate for the office of Supervisor at the ensuing election, subject to the will of the Republican County Convention. JOHN MONTGOMERY.

MURDERED FOR HIS MONEY.

An American Foully Murdered In Sonora.

September 8, 1888.

Information was received at the Epitaph office this morning to the effect that last Sunday or Monday, Charles Jones, a former resident of this place, was brutally murdered near Santa Anna, in the State of Sonora. This is a small Mexican town on the A. & N. M. road, about twenty miles from Magdalena, to which place his body was taken and buried. He left here about two weeks ago intending to go to Altar for the purpose of purchasing a band of horses. He was evidently waylaid and murdered for his money and possessions, as his wounds, three in number, were from a rifle, all showing that he was shot from behind. His money, horse, arms and equipments, and most of his clothes were taken by the assassins. He formerly worked for John H. Slaughter, and also worked hauling wood for Mr. Johnson of Bisbee. He was a very industrious, hard-working man, and was highly esteemed by those who knew him. It is not known whether he has any relations in this country or not, but it is believed he has in Missouri, where he owned considerable landed property. No clue has yet been found as to who committed the deed.

ROBBERY.

A Miner Relieved Of $137 in Cash And His Blankets.

September 18, 1888.

On the night of the fire, a miner living on Toughnut street, being roused by the pistol shots and bell, came up to lend a helping hand in trying to extinguish the conflagration. On returning to his cabin about four o'clock in the morning he found that some miscreant had entered his room and robbed him of $137 in money, two pair of blankets and a gold watch chain. The thief's intention, no doubt, was to steal the blankets, but in taking them off the bed, the purse containing the money (paper and gold) rolled out and he found more spoils than he had counted on. The chain was lying on a table, which he also converted. The gentleman was on the eve of starting to Sonora to work some mining property, and he feels the loss heavily. We hope the scoundrel may be caught and receive his just deserts. We suppress the name of the gentleman by request.

It is said by cattle men that Norton & Goldman will clear $20,000 on their San Carlos beef contract this year.

Mrs. Frank Leslie is somewhat better to-day than she was yesterday.

$250 REWARD.

January 31, 1887.

The Sheriff of the County of Cochise is hereby authorized to offer a reward for the arrest and conviction of the party or parties who attempted to kill J. S. Clark and wife on the evening of January Fourth, eighteen eighty-seven.

(signed) John H. Slaughter,
Sheriff.

Since the killing of two Chinaman in a mysterious manner, one in Tucson and the other in Nogales, the mongolian store keepers are arming themselves for self protection.

FATAL SHOOTING.

Charley Smith Fatally Shot By Charley Cunningham.

September 24, 1888.

On Sunday morning, about half-past twelve, four shots were heard in the vicinity of the Pony saloon, and Charley Smith lay on the side-walk, shot through the thigh. There has been bad blood existing between Cunningham and Smith for about three years, when they had a little difficulty resulting in Smith shooting Cunningham through the foot, in front of what is now the Can Can restaurant, and about one hundred feet from where the shots occurred Sunday morning. On Saturday night Smith met Cunningham in the French wine house, and they renewed their quarrel, when, it is reported, Smith made a gun play at Cunningham, who was unarmed, tried to avoid the quarrel. Weiser then appeared and persuaded Smith to go home, and Smith and Bob Hatch started down the street, and stepped in the Pony saloon. Cunningham in the meantime was talking to some friends, and said he wanted to leave town but was afraid to go out unarmed, and wanted to borrow a pistol. Lazard, one of the party, said he would lend him his, if Cunningham would go to his room. They then started for Lazard's room, Cunningham promising to leave town early the next morning. What transpired from that time until Cunningham came through the Willows saloon is not known, but it is certain that Cunningham secured Lazard's gun, and as he came out of the Willows. Smith standing in front of Marks & Wittig's barber shop, talking to Jack Billaney; Cunningham said, "Charley, does it go," and commenced to shoot. It is not known whether the first shot struck Smith or not as the shooting was very fast, but Smith rolled off the side-walk, with an ugly wound through the thigh. Cunningham was immediately arrested and placed in the county jail.

Cunningham will have a preliminary examination on the tenth of October, or as soon as the result of the wound is determined.

At this writing Smith is very low and is not expected to recover.

WHITE CHAPEL.

Have We A Fiend In Tombstone?

December 23, 1888.

On Wednesday night or rather Thursday morning about two o'-clock, a man knocked at the door of a woman living just above Pasquale Nigro's saloon, on Allen street, and was admitted. On crossing the threshold he assaulted the woman, knocking her down, and after convincing himself that she was prostrated he left the house. The following night a woman living next door to the assaulted woman, named Jesefa, was aroused from her slumbers by a knock at the door. She enquired who was there and was answered back that the door must be opened or it would be broken down. The woman becoming frightened opened the door, and a man entered who with a blow of his fist knocked the woman down and stood over her. For a moment she was stunned, but recovering her senses rose to her feet just as the fiend started to go, she started after him, when he turned and struck her with a knife just on the bridge of her nose, glancing off and cutting her through the nose and under the eye, making an ugly wound. The man turned away and the woman ran into Nigro's saloon bleeding profusely. Dr. Fetterman was called and sewed up the wound. From the description, the same man committed the assault the night previous. What his object was it is unable to discern, and the affair has created the most intense excitement in the neighborhood.

Prospector
February 5, 1903

LEW COFFEE

GENFRAL MERCHANDISE

—AND—

HOME BAKERY.

Fresh Bread a Speciaity. Pastry of all kinds made to order. Brand new stock and lowest prices in the city.

FREMONT STREET NEAR CORNER FIFTH

Miss Gertrude C. Kirwin,
Teacher of Piano.

After Feb. 1st Miss Kirwin will receive pupils in Piano. Special attention paid to proper development of technic by best methods.

CALL ON OR ADDRESS
Cor. 1st and Toughnut Sts.

Prospector
April 12, 1889

NEW YORK

Restaurant,

Allen Street, between Fifth and Sixth

TOMBSTONE, A. T.

OTTO GEISENHOFER, Prop.

Meals from 25c. Up.

The Coolest Place in Town.

FIRST-CLASS IN EVERY WAY.

April 12, 1889

FRENCH WINE HOUSE

609 Allen St., Bet, 6th and 7th.

French Wine, California Claret and White Wine.

MELLWOOD WHISKY,

Spring of 1881, by the bottle or gallon

Alfalfa baled hay 1c per lb.

E. LENORMAND . . . Prop'r

Prospector
February 5, 1903

There are few places in Arizona where there is as large a stream of water going to waste as is now being allowed to run down the gulch just west of town. The water comes from the mines and there is something over 1,000,000 gallons allowed to wind its way toward the San Pedro river daily

Tombstone has the honor of having the largest pump at work in its mines than any other camp in the territory. The volume of water now handled is something over a million gallons every twenty-four hours.

WOMAN KILLED.

Drunken Brawl At Leslie Ranch.

Prospector, July 11, 1889.

William Reynolds came in from Horseshoe Alley, in the Swisshelm mountains this afternoon and reported that last night Frank Leslie, well known in Tombstone as a hard character, had shot a woman supposed to be his wife, and a young man by the name of James Neal. The latter is seriously wounded, being shot through the left arm and below the breast.

It is not known how badly the woman is hurt. Leslie was still on the fight and acting like a crazy man when Reynolds left this morning in quest of a surgeon. Leslie was drunk and had been seeking a quarrel in the valley for some time. Dr. Goodfellow left on horseback immediately for the scene of the shooting. Deputy Sheriff Shattuck telegraphed Slaughter at Bisbee who has sent officers to arrest Leslie.

Prospector, July 12, 1889.

Dr. G. E. Goodfellow returned this morning from Leslie's ranch, after being in the saddle almost continuously for eighteen hours, and traveling over ninety miles. He arrived at the ranch last night, found the woman dead where she fell and Neal suffering from wounds in the arm and body.

Neal was placed in a spring wagon and brought into town where a Prospector reporter found him this afternoon resting as easily as could be expected under the circumstances. He welcomed the intruder, with whom he had been acquainted several years, with pleasure and gave an account of the trouble.

Leslie and Mollie Williams had returned from Tombstone and had been home for one night previous to the one on which the tragedy had occurred. They both had been drinking heavily during this time and had quarreled incessantly. He slapped her and knocked her down several times during the day and said he was going up to Reynolds' place to kill Reynolds but came back about an hour after saying that Reynolds would not fight.

This was toward evening. Both the woman and Neal were sitting outside the house and Leslie began quarreling with the woman. He took another drink and then started from his seat saying, "I'll put a stop to all this," rushed into the house and came back with a Colt's pistol; took deliberate aim at the woman and fired.

"Don't be afraid, it's nothing," said Leslie, and Neal believed that he was only fooling and that he had not been hurt until he felt the blood running down his body. He then started and ran, glancing around but once to see the unfortunate woman run around the house and fall at the back door.

Neal sat dumfounded for a moment only, for Leslie ran to him, placed the gun close to his chest and fired.

Before reaching Reynolds' place he fell and remained there all night. After he had reached Reynolds the next morning, Leslie came there and asked for him saying he wanted to kill him. Neal saw him coming, picked up a shotgun and waited in the tent for him to come, but Leslie went away believing he was not there.

On the way in this morning, Goodfellow and Neal saw Leslie sitting in front of the house at Abbott's ranch and informed Undersheriff Shattuck of the fact and Ben James and Deputy Long started after him. A short distance out they met Taylor and Heine, who were on their way in and Frank Leslie riding with them, he was on his way in to give himself up, he said, and entered the buggy with the two officers who brought him to the county jail.

To our reporter who visited him at the jail he said he was sick. "Oh, my head is sick and wants a rest," he said, and then began to cry. He claims to remember nothing of the affair.

A dirg knife was found in Frank Leslie's cell in the county jail here about two weeks before he was tried and convicted. How it got there is a mystery.

RICHARDS' DEATH.

He Dies Sunday Morning Without Regaining His Reason.

February 3, 1890.

The horrible crime committed in the heart of the city by which Al Richards met an untimely death at the hands of a midnight assassin is still the topic of conversation in all circles. In the history of this city no crime was ever committed, so atrocious and cold blooded in its nature. As mentioned in Saturday's Epitaph Drs. Goodfellow and Huse performed the operation of raising the skull off the brain of the unconscious victim, in the hope that he would rally and at least be able to talk and tell something that could be used as a clue to ferret out the assassin. The operation was successfully performed, and although the most careful nursing and attendance was given him, he breathed his last twelve hours after the operation was performed, without uttering a word. As he breathed his last he attempted to say something, but the sentence died before he had completed it and was unintelligible.

Little knots of people gathered around the scene of the crime and discussed the probability of ever discovering the murderer. Various rumors were afloat, and two or three parties were placed under arrest but released after becoming convinced that they could not have been implicated.

The body was removed to the undertaking rooms of Watt & Tarbell, where Dr. Goodfellow examined the head of the deceased. After the scalp was removed it was evident that the blow that caused the death of Richards was dealt with the blunt end of the axe, as stated in the Epitaph. The blow must have been a terrible one, and given with the intent to kill on the spot. The entire skull was cracked, and the scar on the forehead was but a slight evidence of the deadly work. All over the top and back of the head the skull was cracked open in many places, while the wound in the forehead fitted the blunt end of the axe that had been found by the bedside of the murdered man.

C. S. Fly photographed the head after the scalp had been removed, and nothing has been or will be left undone by the friends of the deceased to bring to justice the perpetrator of the most diabolical murder ever committed in Tombstone.

A Mexican youth, aged about fourteen, was taken to the hospital yesterday by Chief of Police Bravin, having been found lying on the street in a helplessly intoxicated condition. The youth, after being revived, told how he and two other Mexican boys found a flask of whisky in an empty building and drank of the contents. The oldest boy, aged about eighteen, encouraged his comrades to drink, the result being the narrator was left temporarily helpless. The youngest one of the three apparently partook of very little of the liquor. The oldest boy is now in jail and the matter is being investigated today.

$500 Reward.

In accordance with a resolution passed by the Board of Supervisors Feb. 10, 1890, I hereby offer a reward of Five Hundred Dollars for the arrest and conviction of the murderer or murderers of

DAVID D. DUNCAN,

who was killed in the Huachuca mountains on or about January 25th, 1890.

JOHN H. SLAUGHTER,
Sheriff.

Dated Tombstone, Feb. 11, 1890.

Prospector May 6, 1890

In 1884 the Great Register made it appear that John Montgomery was born in Canada. This was a crime that our supervisor was tried for a few years ago and acquitted. After hunting through all of the sins that human flesh is heir to, the Mud Slinger's Association of Tombstone have been obliged to fall back on the old device of taking the unmanly advantage of a typographical error in the Great Register of 1884, whereby the recorder, in copying the registration blanks, made it appear that Mr. Montgomery was born in Canada, when the blank which is on file at the recorder's office states explicitly that he was born in the United States. The association might have retained this mud ball for some other use if they had but cared to investigate the matter. The Great Register shows many inaccuracies which the association might with equal justice use for targets. There are instances of where a man has grown from 40 years of age in '84 to 27 in '86. The M. S. A. should not overlook such glaring errors as this in their hunt for fresh victims.

$500 Reward.

In accordance with a resolution passed by the Board of Supervisors Feb 10, 1890, I hereby offer a reward of Five Hundred Dollars for the arrest and conviction of the murderer or murderers of

ALFRED RICHARDS,

who was killed in Tombstone, Cochise county, Arizona, on the night of January 31st, 1890.

JOHN H. SLAUGHTER,
Sheriff.

Dated Tombstone, Feb. 11, 1890.

1890

New and Second-Hand

Furniture,

CROCKERY
GLASSWARE,
Stoves and House Furnishing Goods.

Highest price paid for second-hand Furniture and goods of all descriptions.

Goods sold 20 per cent cheaper than any other store in town. Call and be convinced.

CURBY & CO.

506 ALLEN STREET.

Proprietors.

THIRD GRAND

Annual Ball.

—BY—

Protection Hose Co No 3

—TO BE GIVEN AT—

MINING EXCHANGE HALL.

—ON—

MAY 1st, 1891.

RECEPTION COMMITTEE

Geo Osbern,	J Shaughnessy,
Joe Lippert,	L Graf,
B Hattich,	J Miano,
P Seamans,	B Hyde
J Prinderville,	Guy Powell.
E Sydow,	Wm Kirlew,
Geo Page,	Jno Blewett,
Frank Ryan,	R W Wood,
Geo Myers,	Ben Cook,
A H Emanuel,	M T Williams,
J P McAllister,	W C Read,
C E Frederick,	W F Bradley,
T A Atchison.	Jno Montgomery.

FLOOR COMMITTEE:

Fred Herrera,	Robt Hennessy,
Wm Shanley,	Ed Whinnen,
Geo Page,	Jno Blewett,
Wm King,	J Welch,
S C Bagg,	Frank Hare.

Floor Manager—J. P. Waters.

ADMISSION, - - *$1.00*
(Admitting gentleman & Ladies.)

All firemen requested to appear in uniform.

BILLIARD PARLORS

A. WENTWORTH, Prop.

AGENT FOR

Anheuser Busch Beer

THE ARCADIA SALOON.

JAS. HAGAN, Prop

Choicest Wines, Liquors and Cigars. Every attention and courtesy shown to patrons.

NEXT DOOR TO CAN CAN.

THE ARIZONA CLUB.

SCHETTER & BERTINI, Props.

Wines, Liquors and Cigars.

"The Best, and Only the Best is our Motto."

Allen Street, Near Fifth.

ANOTHER VICTIM.

FRANK GATCHUM KILLED BY APACHES ACROSS THE LINE.

One Of Durkee's Big Teaming Outfits Attacked Near Oso Negro.

June 7, 1891.

As predicted in last night's EPITAPH the Apaches have added another to their many victims. This time it is a Tombstone boy and how it happened than two toerhs who were with him, but not suffer is a mystery.

The news was received this afternoon by E. G. Gage in the shape of a telegram from Arispe signed by Jim Kirk, in which it was stated that on June third wwhile on the way, to the Oso Negro mine and in the canyon about 15 miles from there, the outfit was attacked by Apaches and Frank Catch team and goods were safe. This is all the information that will be at hand until the stage comes up.

Catchum was a young man about 27 years of age and had been in the employment of J. E. Burke of late and formerly of the Snake Ranch Company.

The attack was made in the morning from which it is inferred that young Catchum was cooking breakfast and was the first man up which gave the other two men, George Thompson and Morg. Hudspeth, a warning and probably saved the entire outfit. The outfit consisted of two large freighting wagons in two trains of three wagons each, pulled by 16 mules. The freight consisted of general mining supplies, among which was 5000 pounds of giant powder. It would seem that the two men must have made their fight away from the wagons from the fact that if a fight from the wagons had been the case, a stray bullet would have in all probability exploded the powder as was done a few years ago near San Carlos.

Mr. Kirk in all probability went to notify the authorities at Arispe and if pursued the band of Indians will make for Arizona. It behooves ranchers to look out for any signs of them and be on guard.

The Epitaph doesn't mind 18 year olds having a vote. But what bugs this weekly newspaper is the 50,000 absentee ballots from Canada.

Mr. Barton Of Prescott.

July 6, 1892

Jerry Barton, the hero of many a shooting and cutting scrape in Cochise county, is one of the leading Republican citizens of Prescott. The Journal-Miner says that Jerry is as firm in his Republicanism as he is in physical structure. He has made a bet that Harrison will be elected or else he will saw ten cords of wood on the plaza. The loser of the bet is to purchase the wood and after it is cut it goes to the winner. Jerry has had this unique proposition from a lean and lanky Democrat under consideration for some time, and it was only after much persistency from his opponent, his fidelity to the cause cropped out in "P-a-r-d-n-e-r, I'll g-o you! S-h-a-k-e."

There's no fool like an old fool – you just can't beat experience.

ANOTHER VICTIM.

"Doc" The Chinaman Is On The Divide With Four U.S. Bullets In His Body.

July 1, 1891

Almost a week has passed and no account of depredations by Apaches have been brought in. People who had lived on the border for ten years were getting restless. The expression of their faces denoted that there was something wrong. But the suspense is all over now. The news was brought in last night that the regular weekly sacrifice had been made and that "Doc" the old Chinaman who had been at the Cananea mines since they were worked in the early eighties, had been riddled with Apache bullets.

A Mexican brought the news in from there to the custom house yesterday and a team at once left for the scene, to bring the man in. A team also left here today to bring the wounded man to Tombstone from the custom house. It is altogether probable that the Chinaman will be dead before assistance arrives as he has four bullet wounds in his body, one of the missiles passing through his neck. The Mexican who brought the news in states that there five Indians in the party and that they left the Chinaman for dead.

The first news of the shooting came to Tombstone last night and was brought in by two of B. F. Packard's herders, and the arrival of the stage today from Oso Negro corroborated their account of the affair.

KILLED.

July 12, 1891.

Manuel Elias Blown To Pieces By A Premature Blast.

Yesterday morning an accident occurred in the Telephone mine which ended the life of Manuel Elias. John Healy and San Sullivan, assisted by two Mexicans, one of whom was named Manuel Elias, were working the mine. Manuel asked whether he could not work on Sunday as he needed all the money he could make to support his family. He was told he could suit himself, and yesterday morning he and his companion went to work.

Manuel was working on the lower level while his companion was on the level above. They had been at work but twenty minutes when a blast went off down below. Manuel's partner, thinking that something was the matter, went down and found the unfortunate man lying upon the bottom of the shaft, dying. He immediately gave the alarm and Dr. Goodfellow was summoned.

John Healty was the first to get to the mine and found Manuel dead The fatal wound was just over the heart. A piece of rock had passed through, breaking a rib and had just bruised the heart, but not penetrating it. Hid body from his thighs up was filled with small pieces of manganese while his face was black with it. He had evidently crawled away from face of place where he had been working, but his sufferings could not have been long.

An examination of the cause of the explosion demonstrated that he had been tamping a hole. A gad was found which bore evidence of having been in close proximity to the point of the explosion, and his left hand was shattered to pieces. It is believed that one shot which had been put off the night previous had blown out, breaking a little rock at the mouth and that Manuel was attempting to reload the hole which was short, with the gad for a tamping rod when the explosion took place. A short hole was still to be found which was in the exact position to have inflicted the injuries.

Manuel remained on the mine before going home the night previous with the rest of the men until the shots went off, and all hands are certain that neither hole which he had charged had missed.

The deceased was the father of four children and was a devoted husband and father. He was a relative of the well known family of the same name which has identified itself with the growth of northern Sonora. Telegrams were sent announcing his death to them.

April 28, 1888

Notice.

Notice is hereby given that all property holders whose names appear upon the delinquent tax roll that the district attorney has entered suits against the same and judgment will be prayed on Monday, May 14. All who previous to that date pay their taxes with one dollar ($1) additional cost, will be exempt from execution and released from suit.

J. V. Vickers,

County Treasurer and Ex-officio Tax Collector.

VIRGIL EARP, in his story published in the Examiner, says that Frank Stilwell, in his dying statement, admitted the killing of Morgan Earp. Without any desire to irritate Mr. Earp, we nevertheless cannot help expressing astonishment that a man, with two pounds of buckshot in his stomach, four bullets in his heart, and his head mutilated by lead beyond recognition, could have had either time or inclination to make any statement whatever.

Mrs. Virgil Earp

Funeral services for Mrs. Virgil Earp, 98, who died Friday, will be conducted at 2 p.m. tomorrow in the Ivy Overholtzer Mortuary Chapel. She was the last of the renowned law-enforcement family of western frontier days. Her husband, who died 40 years ago, was a deputy to his brother, U.S. Marshal Wyatt Earp, credited with cleaning the Clanton gang out of the Tombstone (Ariz.) area. Mrs. Earp was a native of Council Bluffs, Ia. For the last four decades she made her home with her grand-niece, Mrs. C. E. Halliwell, 6301 Eighth Ave.

TOMBSTONE EPITAPH.

JULY 26. 1891

At a place called Tiff city a crowd of toughs attacked a church, knocked the minister down and one of the elders turned loose with an Allen's pepper box, killing one tough and wounding another. After the trouble was over the minister preached the funeral service over the dead tough and he was buried back of the church before he had grown cold and this did not happen in Arizona.

Someone remarks that Tombstone is a virgin camp, to which another rascal answers "Yes, she's been a vergin on a boom for 5 years."

Joe Bignon has sold his theater in Phœnix for $100. Theaters evidently are not appreciated in the Salt river valley when they sell at that figure.

"Saddest Chapter" in History Of Tombstone's Fires Kills Two

(Epitaph, May 15, 1892)

The saddest chapter in Tombstone's history of fire was finished this morning when the firemen who had hastened in answer to an alarm from Engine House No. 1, rushed into the building in season only to rescue two lifeless bodies.

At about 5 o'clock this morning the flames were seen issuing from the residence of Samuel M. Barrow on Toughnut street and pistol shots were fired and the alarm quickly sounded. Meanwhile the unconscious family were fast asleep, little dreaming of the horrible fate so soon to overtake them.

The first to awaken was Miss Lydia Blair, a sister of Mrs. Barrow, who sprang out of bed and opened the door of her room only to be met by a dense volume of smoke. She hastily gave the alarm, and seizing a child in her arms, rushed out of the burning building. Half dazed with smoke and flames, which now seemed to envelop the whole house, Mr. Barrow succeeded in getting his wife who had been ill for some time, and one child to a place of safety, when he realized that his little boy, Sam and Albert Blair, his wife's brother, were yet inside the burning building and rushed frantically back to the rescue.

Before he reached the house, however, Mr. Hattich had dashed fearlessly into the flames and, barely escaping with his own life, brought out the lifeless body of little Sam, who had evidently perished from suffocation. Attention was also turned to the rescue of Albert Blair, whose sleeping apartment was in the eastern portion of the house. An entrance was speedily effected through the wall of the house, and Frank Ryan was the first to rush in. Kneeling by the side of his bed, was found the lifeless body of the young man who doubtlessly barely realized his peril before being rendered insensible by suffocation.

May 1, 1880

New Bank.

Mr. Chas. Hudson, manager for Safford, Hudson & Co., of Tucson, was in town this week and arranged for the establishment of a branch of their banking house in Tombstone. A convenient and desirable location has been secured on Fifth Street, in the new Vizina Block, which will be ready for occupation in a few days. The safe, vault doors, time lock, stationery, etc., has already been shipped from San Francisco. This will be a convenience as well as a benefit. Success to the enterprise.

TOMBSTONE PROSPECTOR

MAY - - - 17, 1893

James Young was placed under $100 bonds by Justice Duncan yesterday to keep the peace for six months. Jim had been reported as having wished citizen Shuster a short life on several occasions since the latter hurled a chunk of ore at his head a few days ago.

The Christiansen Case.

At 7 o'clock this evening the coroner's jury will convene and arrive at a verdict in the case of the death of Christina Christiansen. The young man, Yendresen, who was arrested last night was admitted to bail, but again arrested and held over without bail. He spent the night in jail. His friends say that he is entirely innocent and those who are well acquainted with him scout the idea of his being guilty of such a crime as poisoning a person especially one of his own relatives. Circumstances however warranted the authorities in taking the steps they have taken.

A letter found on a shelf in in the house of deceased written in Norwegian on the reverse side of the sheets torn from a calendar was translated today. It was from the deceased to her mother in which she declines an invitation to visit her parents and tells of her trials and the outlook for the future which is not a gloomy picture.

The first case Miss Sarah Herring had in her career as an attorney, was before the Probate Judge in the case of Walsh vs. Haberlin in which a will was sought to be broken. A decision was given in her favor and the case was appealed to the district court by Allen English attorney for Walsh. Judge Sloan sustained the ruling of the court below in favor of Haberlin, whose attorney Miss Herring was.

DESERTION.

I hereby warn the public not to trust my wife "Flossie" on my account, as she has left my bed and board, and I will not be responsible for *any* debts she may contract.

LOUIS BLONBERG.

Dated Tombstone, January 14, 1890.

Sudden Inspiration.

Allen English went to Tucson today. A sudden inspiration struck him after the stage pulled out and he started for the railroad with a private team.

–The Epitaph, March 14, 1894.

J. YONGE,

Druggist,

ALLEN STREET,

Between Fourth and Fifth Sts.

Drugs and Chemicals

Patent Medicines, Perfumeries, Toilet Articles

PRESCRIPTIONS CAREFULLY PREPARED.

DEAD IN BED.

Mrs. John Miller Breathes Her Last Under Sad Circumstances.

January 29, 1895.

A coroner's inquest was held this morning at the rooms of Justice Alvord over the remains of Mrs. John Miller. The story of her death is told in the words of Wm. Staehle, the principal witness.

He stated that as he was entering his house or office last night quite late a figure passed him and said "good evening." He responded, and upon recognizing her, said "Good evening, Mrs. Miller." She stopped and asked if he had anything to drink. He said he had, and went in, and she followed.

He produced a bottle of whiskey. She declined to take any, but asked if she might rest herself on his bed. He consented, and she threw herself across the top of the bed and went to sleep.

Being tired and sleepy himself, he laid down on the bed also and slept until about four o'clock this morning, when he awoke, and for the first time realized that some one was beside him. He thought it was Frank Broad, and spoke to him. Receiving no answer, he felt over with his hand, and then became aware he was beside a corpse. He arose and notified the authorities.

Dr. Holcombe testified that he had made an examination of deceased, and that she had died of alcoholism. The verdict of the jury was to the same effect.

Her husband was very sick, and is yet unable to go out.

Mrs. Miller had lived in Tombstone for twelve years, and was an honest, hard-working woman, but addicted to strong drink. She was fifty-nine years of age.

The funeral will take place tomorrow afternoon at two thirty o'clock from the Tarbell undertaking parlors.

OUR NELLIE.

February 19, 1895.

A writer for the New York Sun has contributed an article on Nellie Cashman, which will bear repeating. How near it comes to the likeness of our Nellie the reader can judge:

"When only about seventeen years old, she left her home at Dodge City, Kansas, and went to Tucson. This was nine years ago. She got to examining the ore as it came in out of the Tucson mines, and was soon as good a judge of its value as her brother Jim, who was foreman and mineralogist in one of them. The boys in the Tombstone locality pretty soon began betting on her judgment, and found that she was a wonderfully good guesser, and hit it close about every time. Her fame spread, and miners, who are always superstitious, got an idea that to have her around and get her good opinion some way brought good luck. She knew where to dig for ore, too, and some of the ore in the Contention was found by following her advise in running a drift.

Over in Graham county she made a hit one day on copper, and when she went to Tombstone afterward she passed her judgment on some mines there. Bill Wiggins sold the Excelsior and Grand View mines on her advice, and the only dividend they ever yielded was the fifteen thousand dollars he got from them. Other mines were bought after she had examined and reported favorably on them. They are good paying properties now. In Tucson, Bisbee, Tombstone, and other camps, Miss Cashman has conducted general stores and big lodging houses for the miners. She was also in business at Castle Dome. She has had so much experience that she almost invariably turns it to good account, getting town lots, placer sites and load claims for next to nothing, and unloading at a big profit. At first she did not get out of the camp soon enough. Consequently she has been many times rich and poor.

She has indomitable pluck, though and if she goes broke in one place she soon makes a turn and gets up again. Miss Cashman is a rather tall, dark-eyed girl. Going about among the mines, or climbing the hills for outcropings, she wears heavy shoes and strong bloomers, usually covered with a cloak. She is a rapid walker and a quick talker. She is considerable of a reader. She was the first woman in the camp of Harqua Hala, where there were over one thousand five hundred men and no other woman."

A BONANZA FIND?

Heavy Rain Bares A Six-Inch Vein Of Precious Stone.

Great Activity Reported At The Camp East Of The Dragoons.

ACCIDENTALLY FOUND

August 20, 1895.

Mayor P. B. Warnekros returned yesterday from Turquois where he had been on a trip to the camp that is now coming into such prominence through the marvelous rich deposits of turquois gems and their intrinsic value.

The Mayor reports much activity and bustle at the camp and a general air of prosperity seems to pervade all who are fortunate enough to be interested in the Gem district of the county. The heavy rain and washout last week at that camp did considerable damage, while again it was a blessing in disguise, inasmuch as the rushing waters uncovered a valuable vein of turquois over six inches wide. The find was discovered in the bottom of a canyon by the swift current washing the dirt away and leaving the ledge bare. This is an important discovery and may lead to larger deposits, also opening up ground that has not yet been prospected.

The heavy rains filled many of the drifts and tunnels on the side of the mountain the water rising higher then it has ever been known before.

At Turquois a large frame house was turned almost end for end by the water and rain, and other pranks are reported. Mr. Goldsmith, brother of Julius Goldsmith now on the grounds and one of the owners of the bonanza group of which Mr. N. C. Roscom is superintendent, is expected to arrive here some time next week to carry into execution the more extensive work which has about been decided upon, and upon his arrival the opening up of the mines and employment of more men is probable.

Regular shipments of ore are being sent to New York by Wells Fargo and Company and one hundred pounds is now ready, after being sorted, to be sent east.

Work on the Parker mines will be resumed on the tenth of next month, when Mr. Parker who is now in Silver City will return. These mines are valuable and have produced many valuable gems. A company is about organized to work this property with a sufficient capital to back them to push work on an extensive scale.

The Holmes mine is looking extra well and will soon rank with the producers.

The lead properties which are being worked at North Camp show immense deposits of this much sought after metal.

A GAY LOTHARIO.

How He Pressed His Suit For The Hand Of A Dusky Maiden.

August 27, 1895.

Early this morning there was a disturbance in the household of a Mexican woman, who lives with her family of four children at the lower end of town, that came very near ending in a tragedy. An ebony-hued countryman who lives in Sonora demonstrated his undying affection for Maria the eldest daughter of the household, to whom he had been paying court for a long time, by attempting to annihilate the whole family after the most approved methods as practiced of late. He started in by demanding of his lady love, whose mother evidently objected to his attention to her daughter, that she return forthwith certain presents he had made to her, and upon refusal to do so he slapped her in the face and struck her with his fist, leaving a bit lump on the back of her head as a mark of affection. He followed this up by an attack upon her mother, who had interposed an objection to his arduous demonstrations of love, and drawing a self-cocking revolver declared that he would kill them both. As he was highly infuriated by this time, it is quite probable that he would have carried his threat into execution had not the mother succeeded in knocking the weapon out of his hand. Meanwhile the girl had run out of the house and her mother followed her as soon as she could get away.

Although much infuriated, the ladies refuse to prosecute or even have arrested their courting friend. The latter left and is probably gone to join the Mexican who recently left the chain gang of Chief Doyle, and are now safe in Mexico.

DESPERATE FIGHT.

SHERIFF FLY AND CHIEF OF POLICE DOYLE HAVE AN EXCITING ENCOUNTER WITH TRAMPS.

Deputy Constable Raney Badly Wounded And One Tramp Killed—Particulars Of The Affair.

December 18, 1895.

Sheriff Fly and Chief of Police, Doyle returned last night from Benson, where they became involved in an exciting and thrilling encounter with hobos, which resulted in the death of one of the traveling gentry and the probable fatal wounding of William Reany, deputy constable at Benson.

It will be remembered that on Tuesday mention was made of some 12 or 15 tramps arriving in Tombstone, but the chief of police cut their visit short and accompanied them to the city limits. The entire number made their way toward the railroad and next heard of them was a telegram to the sheriff's office that a house on the river had been broken into and all moveable effects stolen. Sheriff Fly and Chief Doyle at once left for the scene, and on arriving, found the house ransacked and also a pair of pants, evidently discarded by one of the tramps, which the chief at once recognized as being worn by a particular hard-looking individual who was one of the number in Tombstone, thus giving circumstantial evidence that the robbing was done by the same gang who visited our city, and from other information received two of the number were the ones wanted. The tramps having continued on to Benson, the officers also made for the same point. Here Deputy Constable Raney informed theoffic ers of the whereabouts of the tramps, who had taken possession of a house below town. The three minions of the law arrived and Sheriff Fly stepping to the door asked all to come out.. For reply an empty tomato can, thrown with considerable force, grazed his head and a volley of the vilest epithets greeted his ears.

The vagrants were informed that as an officer of the law they must comply with the request and no trouble would be had if peaceably and obediently met. A piece of wood was hurled through the door in response, followed by an avalanche of the most vulgar experesions. Finally all, with two or three exceptions, were induced

WYATT EARP.

An Indictment In Arizona Still Hangs Over Him.

December 10, 1896

There is on file in the district court of this First Judicial District in and for Pima county an indictment for murder against Doc Holliday, Wyatt Earp, Warren Earp, Sherman McMasters and John Johnson, charging them with the murder of Frank Stillwell in Tucson, March 20, 1882. The Star says this indictment was found and presented to the court March 25, 1882. After the finding of the indictment the parties were outlawed for several months and were never taken. Most of the parties are now dead, but the fact of Wyatt Earp's appearance in the recent Fitzsimmons-Sharkey fight makes the fact one of interest as the indictments stand against him untried or otherwise disposed of.

THE ROBBERS.

Line Rider Robson Is Killed From Ambush.

August 19, 1896.

A telegram from Sheriff Fly was received at the sheriff's office late last night giving the sad news of the death of Line Rider Robson who was with Sheriff Fly's posse while having a fight with the Nogales bank robbers who were trailed to Skeleton canyon near the New Mexican line.

Previous telegrams sent in by courier showed the posse were hot on the trail and gaining on the robbers until last evening unexpectedly the possee, which included Sheriff Fly of Cochise, Sheriff Leatherwood of Pima, Deputies Alvord and Johnson and later joined by Guard Robson, were ambushed, and what transpired is explained in the telegram, which is published herewith and reads as follows:

"Black Jack and gang ambushed us yesterday, evening in Skeleton canyon, killed Robson, custom guard. The first fire killed two horses and wounded another. They got two of our horses, we two of theirs. Think we wounded two, not certain, as they were concealed. It was a stubborn fight.
"FLY AND LEATHERWOOD."

Black Jack referred to is the leader of the cowboys who is believed to have lead the attempted holdup.

The killing of Robson shocked the many friends of the popular and well known guard being well known in Tombstone having lived here with his family for some time. Robson was a young man but 24 years old and leaves a devoted wife and child to mourn his untimely end and in their hour of alliction the community extend their heartfelt sympathy and consolence.

ED SCHIEFFELIN.

Tombstone in Mourning As Prospector-Founder Is Laid To Rest With Simple Rites.

Prospector, May 24, 1897.

The funeral of Ed Schieffelin, the first discoverer of precious metals in the Tombstone district, took place yesterday afternoon from Schieffelin hall.

Sunday, May 23, 1897, will long be remembered by our people. The bells tolled forth the knell of high noon. The day was bright; all nature seemed in harmony with the occasion. The people of towns of our county assembled — Bisbee, Pearce, Wilcox, Benson, and all of the county around-about came to assist at the last sad rites of him they called friend.

Flags were flying at half-mast from the spires of all public buildings and the whole city was in the deepest of mourning for this man who has laid the foundation for the great prosperity and happiness of so many of his fellow creatures. The deceased was a man free from ostentation and although possessed of much worldly goods he was the friend of the worthy poor, ever ready to lend a helping hand to the needy where merit went hand in hand with want. He was a worker himself and had seen the hard side of life, hence could and did appreciate the efforts of the honest struggling poor and was ready and willing to give liberally.

The body had been placed in position and the casket was covered with floral offerings of beautiful designs, the hall being draped in deep mourning. Notice had been given by Mayor Emmanuel requesting the people to turn out enmass to do honor to the departed which was responded to by our entire population; the hall was crowded, many were compelled to remain outside.

They were conducted to seats near the bier while a profound silence fell upon the assemblage.

When the proper time arrived, Col. Wm. Herring, who had known the deceased intimately and well during the period of Tombstone's prosperity, stepped to the platform and with that subdued emotion that seemed to pervade the entire assemblage, delivered an eulogy befitting the character of the man, giving a sketch of his life, the trend of his nature and his determination from boyhood up to be a discoverer; the hardships encountered and the efforts made to turn from his settled course, but all to no purpose; the man pushed on and the mines which not only made the discoverer independent, but enriched thousands of others and upon the output of which a day was founded, and thousands of God's creatures made happy and comfortable as the result of this man's indomitable determination and energy were opened up and a stream of precious metals, which lasted for years, was added to the world's riches.

But the hero had finished his work, he had laid down the pick and had put aside his hammer and canteen, and had taken up his march for other discoveries in a land yet unexplored and from which no reports have ever come.

As he had lived quietly and unobtrusively, so he desired to be buried without pomp or ceremony.

CHINESE GAMBLER.

Arrested For Can Can Robbery.

Epitaph, October 23, 1898.

Last night Mr. Ah Wing, an almond eyed celestial gentleman who presides over the dishwashing department of the Can Can restaurant was arrested by Chief of Police Wiser and booked on a charge of burglary being strongly suspected of robbing the Can Can safe

BRUNCKOW MINE BUILDING IS SAID TO BE HAUNTED

Old Dobe Still Stands in Road to Charleston; Is First Cochise Building

(Tombstone Prospector, May 20, 1897)

The halcyon days of Tombstone are often brought to memory, and if even at the expense of some unfortunate, it is a pleasure to allow the mind to revert back to the 80's when this was surely the greatest mining camp on earth; when the shrill whistles of the numerous mines were deafening to the ear; when the bad man prevailed and the music of his "gun" lulled many to sleep; when bold highwaymen plied when "life" began with the fading away of each day and there was one continial round of pleasure.

Crime then was regarded as a matter of course, criminals held full sway and it was a case of survival of the fittest. These reflections are brought to mind through the report of a spook which has taken possession of a long since abandoned mine, the history of which would at once establish it as the appropriate habitation of ghosts.

In early days the Brunckow mine, three miles below Tombstone, was the scene of much excitement; dissension arose among the owners and shooting affairs became numerous, occasionally a man was missing and that ended it; one man was supposed to have been shot and thrown into a well, but as there were abundant men in those days an investigation was deemed needless.

Five men were found at th Brunckow with their toes pointing heavenward at one time; it was an ideal rendesvouz for the knight of the road, and the five dead men found there were of a party of freebooters who had raided a Wells-Fargo bullion wagon and fought over a division of the spoils.

If such a thing be possible then it is no wonder that the spirit of the departed should linger around the scene of pillage and carnage, and reputable men of Tombstone will vouch for the truthfulness of the statement that the mine is haunted. The story goes that every night can be seen a menacing ghost stalking around and through the dilapidated 'dobe shanty; people have atempted to investigate, but upon approaching apparently near enough to speak, the spook suddenly vanishes, only to appear as quickly at some other point, leading its would-be queriest a lively and illusive chase.

There is apparently but one, and when ot to be seen, mining operations can be heard in the old shaft, pounding on drills, sawing lumber and working along ever and anon just as though silver had never depreciated. That there is some mysterious movements around the Brunckow is honestly believed by many here, and several of our sturdy plainsmen and mountaineers will visit this deserted mine and attempt an investigation.

Editors Note: The old Brunckow House is still standing on the Charleston road and is perhaps the first building ever erected in Cochise county.

July 23, 1882

INTERESTING RELICS.

F. C. Earle, general manager of the El Paso Smelting company, was a Tombstone visitor to-day. Mr. Earle is president of the Hershal Mining company in this district and makes occasional trips here on a visit of inspection.

Mr. Earle, while viewing the large specimen collection and ore cabinet in his former office here, which is one of the attractions of Tombstone and now in charge of Assayer L. Hart, referred to several specimens of pottery and crude relics of prehistoric origin which Mr. Earle had discovered and placed in the cabinet over twenty years ago. Queerly enough, the vicinity in which these relics were found is now the location of the Courtland. Mr. Earle states that he found ruins of what evidently was an Aztec village in the valley near what is now Courtland, and it is not improbable that a thriving settlement existed there during the Aztec period, then passed out of existence, and has again, phenix-like arisen from its ashes.

THE JUDGES CHARGE.

His Instructions and Charge to the Jury.

November 28, 1899.

An exchange says a judge of the old school is said to have once summed up a very complicated case in the following language: "Gentlemen of the jury—You have all heard the evidence, you have also heard what the learned counsel for the plaintiff has told you, your verdict will be for the plaintiff; but if, on the other hand, you believe what the defendant's counsel has told you, then you will give a verdict f or the defendant. But you are like me, and don't believe what either of them has said, then I don't know what you will do."

PEARL HART INNOCENT.

Acquitted by a Pinal County Trial Jury.

November 18, 1899.

A trial jury at Florence must have concluded that Pearl Hart, the former bandit is untruthful and unworthy of belief. She was put on trial Monday for a crime of which nobody imagined there was any doubt of her guilt. The Republican says a letter received at Phenix yesterday said that she had been acquitted. It was also stated that the woman was held on another charge, probably that of interfering with the United States mails.

Pearl Hart, assisted by Joe Boot, held up the Globe-Florence stage near Riverside last June and obtained about four hundred dollars from the passengers. The robbers were traced directly from the their crime to the place of their capture near Benson. The woman confessed her guilt a hundred times, gloried in her exploit and particularly in the circumstance that she was the leader of the expedition, having coaxed and bulldozed Boot into it. Her confessions were published along with her portrait in most of the yellow journals and some of the household magazines between New York and San Francisco. A month ago she broke jail from Tucson,

---

A Mexican youth, aged about fourteen, was taken to the hospital yesterday by Chief of Police Bravin, having been found lying on the street in a helplessly intoxicated condition. The youth, after being revived, told how he and two other Mexican boys found a flask of whisky in an empty building and drank of the contents. The oldest boy, aged about eighteen, encouraged his comrades to drink, the result being the narrator was left temporarily helpless. The youngest one of the three apparently partook of very little of the liquor. The oldest boy is now in jail and the matter is being investigated today.

February 14, 1894.

The pet cat at the Can Can restaurant jumped into the safe unobserved when the door was open and Mr. Walsh's back was turned. The door was closed and the combination turned off. The cat was missed but hunting high and low did not reveal its where abouts. It was given up as lost until the proprietor went to the safe yesterday morning and opened the big door.

Out fell the cat more dead than alive. It was taken to the stove, thawed out and doctored. Its nine lives are gradually coming back to it, and it is safe to say that it has been effectually cured of hiding away in dark corners.

Bucket Of Blood Saloon

PEARCE, ARIZ.

The only second class saloon in the city.

CROWLEY & CO. PROPRIETORS.

October 26, 1882

Our parlours will remain closed for a fortnight following the celebration of week-end last — Our 33 doves are vacationing from the rigors of those three days and the parlours require refurbishing.

A NEW DIET.

Here is Something You Might Take.

February 14, 1899.

In the Medical Age a Chinese gentleman advocates the use of the rat as an article of diet, and makes the following remarks on its properties as a hair restorer: "What the carrot is to a horse's coat, a rat is to the human hair. Neither fact can be explained, but every horseman knows that a regiment of carrots will make his horse as smooth and lustrous as velvet, and the Chinese, especially the women, know that rats used as food stop the falling out of hair and make the locks soft, silky and beautiful. I have seen it tried many times, and every time it succeeded."

SIMPLE MONUMENT OF GRANITE OVER PIONEER'S GRAVE

Schieffelin In Final Rest On Boulder Strewn Hill West Of Tombstone

(Epitaph, Nov. 28, 1899)

A description of the monument, now nearly completed, that is being errected to the memory of Edward Schieffelin by those who were nearest and dearest to his heart while he lived on earth, would not be amiss.

The monument is being built about two and one half miles west of Tombstone, among a lot of huge granite boulders that are scattered all around in a variety of forms and shapes suggestive of a great upheaval such as only scientific men can account for. It was here, on the spot marked by the monument, that Edward Schieffelin, the discoverer of the Tombstone mines, in 1878 made his camp, and fearing an attack by the treacherous Apache Indians, sought refuge and shelter behind these boulders.

The monument has been built of the granite boulders that surround the grave. The design is unique and probably unlike anything ever before built in the United States. It is intended to represent as nearly as possible a monument such as a prospector would build to designate a mining location.

Upon an elevated piece of ground has been constructed a solid granite base consisting of pieces of various size, some weighing over a ton, firmly cemented together, in all having a measurement of twenty feet square.

From the center of this base rises a pedestal, commencing at sixteen feet in diameter at the bottom and tapering gradually to a height of twenty feet in the shape of a cone, the top having a diameter of four feet, which is covered with a large flat slab. On this rests a semi circular boulder of a large size, but not extending to the edge of the slab it sets upon. The entire structure is twenty-five feet in height.

All granite pieces used in the monument have been cut to fit a particular place, but not polished, the intention being to represent the boulders in their natural form as near as possible.

The only finished or dressed stone used in the whole work is a diamond-shaped slab three feet wide set in the pedestal, upon which has been cut the name and date of death, May 12, 1897.

The work is being done by M. W. Jones, of the Tucson Marble Co., and reflects great credit upon his ability and skill as a designer and builder. It will probably be completed within two weeks.

September 28, 1881

The Funeral.

The funeral of the McLowry brothers and Clanton yesterday was numerically, one of the largest ever witnessed in Tombstone. It took place at 3:30 from the undertaking rooms of Messrs. Ritter & Ream. The procession, headed by the Tombstone brass band, moved down Allen street, and thence to the cemetery. The sidewalks were densely packed for three or four blocks. The body of Clanton was in the first hearse, and those of the two brothers in the second, side by side, and were interred in the same grave. It was a most impressive and saddening sight, and such a one as it is to be hoped may never occur again in this community.

The Final Resting Place of Ed Schieffelin

'NEATH this cairn of rocks, erected in the form of a giant prospector's discovery monument, rest the bones of Tombstone's founder, Ed Schieffelin. The monument, located about three miles west of the old mining camp, was erected by friends and associates of the great prospector.

LOST ORE BODY.

Dig In Tombstone Streets For Lost Toughnut Ore Body.

Epitaph, June 28, 1899.

When the Huachuca water pipe line was laid on Allen street one of the laborers, named Gregory, claimed he unearthed a pocket of rich deposit of silver ore. He kept the secret to himself expecting some day to secure a lease on the Toughnut, when he would return to unearth the treasure he accidentally discovered.

The find was made some eighteen or nineteen years ago, and since Gregory has died. Before passing away he disclosed his secret to several friends and the report bearing evidence of authenticity as far as Gregory's revelation is concerned, reached the ear of a chloride here to placed enough credence in the story that he has secured the necessary lease and has begun work on the place supposed to be where the discovery was made.

Gregory stated he uncovered the ore at a point between the Bird Cage and Frederick's tin shop, and the work of digging a ditch to the pipe line between the points named is now in progress.

OFF FOR CHINA

Cochise County Cowboys Who Enlisted In The Service.

August 27, 1900.

Four more well-known Cochise cowboys have enlisted in the U. S. service as packers and are to be assigned for duty to China. The last four to go are Tom Peppers, Horace Williams, Wm. Bennett and Wm. Sanders, all of whom go to Benson to-day and from there by government transportation to San Francisco. From there they expect to ship on the U. S. transport to China by the end of this week.

Last week a party of five other Cochise county cowboys left for San Francisco to report for duty. These five were Lee Ramsey, John Kelly, John Pyeatt, Dan Aston and Wm. Johnson. Cochise county has already furnished over twenty-five packers for service in China and quite a number of others from here are contemplating enlistment to go to the Orient.

The EPITAPH has arranged to receive some letter from the brave Cochise county boys and we expect to publish a few of their interesting latter of things as they view it, within a short time. The best wishes of the many friends of the packers go with them in their new duty.

NEW GOODS AT NEW PRICES!

A. D. OTIS & CO., 414 FREMONT ST.,

Have opened and are offering for sale the LARGEST and MOST ELEGANT STOCK OF GOODS in their lines ever brought to Tombstone, being the result of careful Personal Selection in the Eastern Markets, and bought at a Saving of from Ten to Thirty per Cent. from San Francisco Prices, the benefit of which they will Give their Customers. Their Crockery and other Goods are of the Best Makes. They have Many Novelties in the way of

Elegant Lamps and Chandeliers,

Fine China Ware, Majolica Goods,

Elegant Designs in Glassware, Fine Cutlery,

All the New Designs in Chamber Sets.

Silver Plated Ware,

Everything in Cuspidores, and

Bird Cages in Great Variety.

They have also lately received 100 Packages of Hardware, which makes their Assortment complete; and also added to their assortment a Stock of Willow Ware, and a Stock of

GUNS, PISTOLS, Etc., Etc

The Public are Invited to an Examination of this Stock, in which they will find Good Articles at Moderate Prices.

COME AND SEE!

Ladies of Tombstone and Vicinity.

I am determined to have the Ladies' trade of the town if good new Goods at low prices can procure it. I have just returned from San Francisco with

ALL NEW GOODS.

Ladies' Dress Goods, consisting of fine Black and Colored Silks and Satins of all shades, Watered Silks and Satins for trimmings, Camels' Hair Goods, Poplins, Delains and Merinos. I claim to have the finest lot of GINGHAMS, LAWNS, and PIQUETS in the territory, which I will sell CHEAPER THAN ANY OTHER HOUSE. Of the new styled Spangled Goods I have a complete assortment. Trimmings of all descriptions, Hoop Skirts, Ladies' Hose, Children's Dresses ready made, White Sacks and Aprons, Grenadines and Lace Bunting very nice and cheap. LINEN LACES BY THE WHOLESALE. All I ask is to call and see the entire

New Stock of Goods Just Opened.

CITY OF PARIS DRY GOODS STORE,

Two Doors Below the Cosmopolitan Hotel,

HAWKINS, BOARMAN & CO.,

WHOLESALE DEALERS IN

WINES, LIQUORS, OILS AND CIGARS,

No. 116 Fourth St.

Have a complete stock of WINES, LIQUORS, OILS and CIGARS of the Finest Brands, which they offer to the public at prices to suit the times.

We will confine, ourselves EXCLUSIVELY to the Wholesale Business and trust to this fact, and the good quality and reasonable prices of our goods to obtain a fair share of patronage from the merchants and families of this community.

HAWKINS, BOARMAN & CO.
116 Fourth Street, between Allen and Toughnut.

PEOPLES' STORE

Cor. Fourth and Fremont Streets,
(Formerly Summerfield Bros. Store.)

JUST OPENED--------GOODS ARRIVING EVERY DAY

......CONSISTING OF......

DRY GOODS. LADIES AND CHILDRENS' SHOES, Slippers, Silk Handkerchiefs, Etc Fine assortment of Kid Gloves and in fact everything that can be found in a first-class Dry Goods Store. Ladies Hats.

Gents' Clothing, Furnishing Goods.

Hats, Caps, Boots and Shoes.

Trunks, Valises, and Anything you may Call For.

CARPETS, WINDOW SHADES and WALL PAPER
Which I will Sell at astonishingly Low Prices.

Come and Examine my Stock and Prices Before Purchasing Elsewhere.

Remember the Place---Summerfield's Old Store.

SALA SCHEIN - - Proprietor.

A HOLD UP.

THE N M & A TRAIN HELD UP AT FAIRBANK.

ONE ROBBER IS CAUGHT.

"Three Fingered Jack" Is Wounded And Run Down By Posse.

MESSENGER MILTON SHOT.

February 18, 1900.

Fairbank was the scene of a hold-up last night, three masked men armed to the teeth making a raid on the N. M. & A. train just as the north bound passenger train pulled into and stopped at the station.

The movements of the robbers and their methods would indicate that they were no novices in their work, exhibiting plenty of nerve and reckless courage and during their brief stay made things very exciting, as a hold-up usually is. The robbers secured but little booty for their trouble and although various reports are given out as to the amount of money secured it is authentically stated that but one package, containing seventeen dollars in Mexican money, which happened to be out of the safe in the express car is missing.

The particulars as learned by the Epitaph from several eye witnesses is to the effect that as soon as the train stopped and the agents and helpers were busy unloading and loading mail and express matter, three men were seen to emerge from the side of the depot platform. One of the men went to the engine and the other two hurried to the express car, ordering everybody to throw up their hands and immediately. began shooting by way of enforcing the order. The bystanders. with hands aloft, were somewhat scattered and the leader commanded all to "bunch up" punctuating his remarks with comprehensive prolanity. It is needless to say all hastened to obey. Presently the engineer and fireman came from their post and were marched to the crowd were they were also commanded to remain with hands up. The first robber who stopped at the engine had marched the two railroaders to the crowd at the point of a pistol.

Meanwhile a fussilade of shots was kept up and the mail and express car was perforated with shots. Express Messenger J. D. Milton appeared at the door of his car with a winchester and began firing at the robbers. At the first fire from Milton one of the robbers was positively seen to fall to the ground. Whether he was wounded or not is not known but he returned the fire as did also the others, when suddenly Milton dropped having been shot in the right arm. At this exciting moment the horses on the Tombstone stage, who were nearby, became frightened from the shooting and started to run away. Driver Ed Tarbell, who was in the "bunched" crowd started to head them off when one robber sternly ordered him to halt, Ed wisely halted. Then the robber who had fallen to the ground as stated above, fired several shots at the floeing animals, one bullet taking effect in the stifle of the horse and effectually stopped the runaway although at the probable cost of the horse which may die.

When it was evident that Milton was helpless, one of the robbers climbed into the express car with a sack and hurriedly rummaged through papers, packages, etc. The through safe was locked and but little of value was to be found. Quite a number of things were overlooked in the hurry of the robber and no attempt was made to blow open or have the messenger unlock the iron box. It is said but one package containing seventeen dollars Mexican money is gone, although several bystanders claim the sack was fairly well filled when the robbers left the car.

The leader of the robbers then turned his attention to the depot and inquired of the "crowd" where the agent was. Agent Guy was in the "bunched crowd" but descretly kept silent and none of the others cared to import the set of his whereabouts. With another voluminous outburst of protanity, the robber went to the door of the depot which was locked. He kicked down the door, walked in, found all the safes and drawers locked and came out empty handed. The three robbers then walked off together going west of the depot where it is presumed they had horses ready and in waiting.

The train immediately backed to Benson for medical assistance for Messenger Milton. It is understood the bones in his arm are so shattered that amputation will be necessary. The injury to Milton is to be regretted. He was a brave and efficient officer and well known here.

A Sheriff's posse was organized last night in Tombstone and were at the scene as soon as possible. Trailing was impossible last night as no trails could be found. This morning more officers were sent out and notifications were dispatched in every direction to keep a sharp lookout. No clue whatever is had to the identity of the robbers thus far.

Epitaph, June 2, 1901.

The state makers are between two fires. The republican papers say that if they do not submit a separate article to vote on, which is known as the Mormon test oath, that they will kill statehood. On the other hand, if they do give us the test oath to vote upon, we will not reach the goal for the reason that it will be snowed under, and a republican senate would never let us in with any such democratic dye on us.

THREE FINGERED JACK.

The Bandit Dies From The Effect Of His Wounds.

February 2?, 1900.

Yesterday morning about seven o'clock Jesse Dunlap, known as Three Fingered Jack died at the hospital from the wounds he received while in the hold up at Fairbank last week from the gun in the hands of Messenger Milton.

Three Fingered Jack bore up with remarkable fortitude from his serious wounds. During the last night of his earthly existence he sank rapidly. Though very much weakened he retained consciousness to the last and about one hour before he died he feebly whispered "goodby" to his nurse.

An effort was made a day or two since to secure the dying statement of Three Fingered Jack but the latter confidently stated that he was not going to die yet and refused to make any confession. It is known however, that the wounded robber subsequently made a "clean break" of the affair and "squealed" on his pals for the inhuman treatment in leaving him alone, helpless and wounded, to die on the desert.

Dr. Walter held a post mortem examination on the body of deceased and extracted three buckshot from his body. The wound which undoubtedly caused death was the bullet which penetrated the abdomen and ranged so as to pass through the liver, ledging in the back bone. A coroners jury was summoned and returned a verdict of death by gunshot wounds at the hands of Messenger Milton while in the defense of W. F. and Company property.

The body of Three Fingered Jack was buried to-day at the cemetery his interment being had at the cost of the county.

JAIL DELIVERY.

Wm. Stiles, Turned States Evidence, The Liberator.

DEPUTY BRAVIN SHOT.

BURT ALVORD, BRAVO JOHN AND STILES GET AWAY--POSSE IN PURSUIT.

OTHER PRISONERS STAY

Halderman Brothers and the Others Choose to Remain—Calmness of the Deputy.

THE PRISONERS' KINDNESS

About three o'clock Tombstone was thrown into a fever of excitement, the like of which has not visited our city since the days of the hanging of Heath by an indignant mob. The occasion for this was the news of a jail break at the county jail and the shooting of Deputy Sheriff George Bravin who was wounded in an attempt to block the break for liberty.

Despite the most precautionary measures taken by the Sheriff's office to guard against any attack of friends of the prisoners in jail on charge of trainrobbery to secure their release by force, as was feared, the expected happened, but from a source that was never suspicioned, the dastardly work being done by William Stiles, the self confessed train robber who turned states evidence against his pals, then further proved his treachery by attempting to help them escape from jail, even at the sacrifice of the lives of any who might stand in the way. Fortunately the brave Deputy Sheriff, George Bravin, was not killed though he had a most narrow escape.

Last evening Matt Burts was brought over from the Tucson jail for his preliminary examination here for trainrobbery. William Stiles the principal witness who turned states evidence, also arrived to testify. It was deemed advisable by the authorities and prosecution not to place Burts in jail in company with the other prisoners on some charge for reasons that are obvious. As a consequence Burts was under guard of two deputies. His trial was to be had to-day and again to be taken to the Tucson jail to-morrow.

While the guards were away from the jail with Burts, Deputy Sheriff Bravin was left alone in charge of the jail. William Stiles, who, up to this time had helped the officers in every way to prosecute his pals, and who was believed to be the last man to even think of aiding in a jail break, suddenly pushed a six shooter at Deputy Bravin, while in the front jail room and commanded him to deliver the keys of the jail. Bravin was unarmed, having left his gun on the office desk, while stepping temporarily into the jail room. Instead of complying, Bravin pluskily knocked at the pistol of his assailant. At the same time Stiles shot and the Deputy fell. Stiles in an instant secured the keys and opened the main cell doors inviting all the prisoners to make a break for liberty. Burt Alvord and "Bravo John" both charged with trainrobbery came out, and rushing to the front with Stiles, took three Winchester rifles and two six shooters, the whereabouts of which was known to Stiles, and hurriedly left, the three going down Fremont street to the ranch of John Escapule below town where they stole two horses, grazing near, and rode off toward the Dragoons two of the men riding one horse.

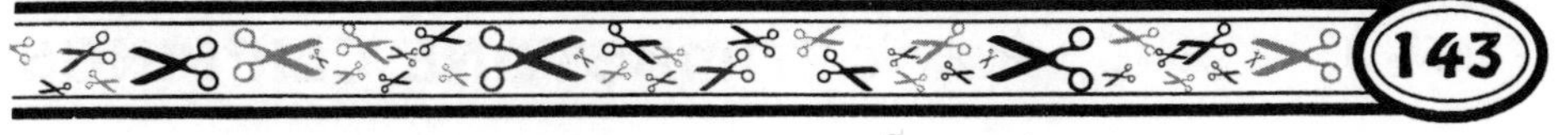

The opportunity of escape was offered the entire twenty four prisoners in jail. As the Halderman brothers came out Deputy Bravin spoke to them saying kindly that they better not attempt escape as they would not have time to get away. Both of the condemned men said: "all right, George, we'll stay." William Dawning one of the accused train robbers refused to go at all as was also the case of the Owen brothers under the same charge; Sid Page also remained inside. Several of the other prisoners started to go and one prisoner named Griffith, at the request of the deputy, closed the iron door baring further escape. The coolheadedness of the wounded deputy prevented the escape of the entire twenty four prisoners.

The Halderman brothers seeing the wounded condition of the deputy, together with the other prisoners, carried him to a bed in the ante room and endeavored to relieve his pains.

A few minutes after the escape several posses were in pursuit and are believed to be but a short distance behind the three fugitives. Many determined men offered their services and were sent out. The feeling runs high and should the escaped be recaptured the probability for a lynching is exceedingly good.

Bravin is shot through the calf of his leg the bullet passing below his knee, through the leg and taking off two toes on his other foot. He is resting easy at his home under the medical care of Doctor Walter.

Up to time of writing no news from the posses has been had.

HORSE TRIAL.

Territory of Arizona vs. Rocking HZ.

One of the strangest trials in western jurisprudence was the trial and sentencing of a brown horse in the Fairbank justice court June 25, 1906.

Fairbank, on the San Pedro river nine miles from Tombstone, was a lively mill town, and Tombstone's shipping point both for the El Paso & Southwestern railroad toward Tucson and the Santa Fe branch to Nogales.

According to documents belonging to Mr. and Mrs. S. T. Lindley Sr., the case of the "Territory of Arizona vs. One Brown Horse Branded Rocking HZ on Left Shoulder" is as follows:

The horse was seized by Porter MacDonald, deputy quarantine inspector, and accused of straying on the public domain. Held for trial, MacDonald was the complaining witness. The poor horse was not represented by counsel and was sentenced to be sold at public auction July 17, 1906.

Sufferers of Gleeson Fire

June 15, 1912

Twenty-eight buildings and contents with an estimated total value of more than $100,000 is the losses of the Gleeson fire last week.

B. A. Taylor stated that he would be looser to the extent of $85,000 over and above his insurance of $10,000 which was the only insurance carried on the portion of the camp that was destroyed.

G. I. Van Meter estimated his property loss on seven buildings, as being $2500.

Juan Assad stated that his loss on stock, with $365 in currency, amounted to $2500.

Mike Simon stated that his loss on stock was $1700 besides $375 in currency that was burned.

No Heart is Tortured.

Tonight there will undoubtedly be a packed house at the Crystal Palace to see Virginia Pearson in "A Tortured Heart," not so much that the people want to see anybody's heart tortured, but simply because it is pay day at the mines.

On tomorrow night the Sunday attraction will be Mildred Holmes in "The Courage of the Common Place," and a good house will see that.

On Monday night Fanny Ward will be seen in "The Crystal Gazer."

The cozy little Crystal will have three good houses, as all plays are up to the ordinary standard of the house.

–The Epitaph, Jan. 6, 1918.

HALDERMAN SENTENCE.

August Tenth is Date Set For The Death Penalty.

June 25, 1900.

Last evening the two Halderman Brothers, Thomas and William, were arraigned in court to receive the re-sentence of the death penalty for the murder of Ainsworth and Moore, the supreme court having denied the condemned man a new trial. Beyond the presence of court officers and D. L. Lang, the angle of the condemned men and who has been a source of muchc onsolation and encouragement to the prisoners, but few were present, the arraignment not being generally known.

When asked by the court if the prisoners had any reason to offer why sentence should not be passed, Mark Smith attorney for the prisoners, made a statement recalling the history of the crime. He took occasion to state he found no fault with the court, or make any accusations of unfairness.

He felt, however, that because of the general indignation and feeling existing against his clients, and trial had during the time such feeling was uppermost, may have had some influence on the verdict. He then asked that the sentence be set ahead a sufficeint time to permit the perfection of an appeal to the governor for executive elemency. Judge Davis, in deference to the request, set the date of the death sentence, nearly sixty days hence, fixing it at Friday, August tenth and was so ordered.

The prisoners showed no signs of emotion and did not offer a word. They returned to their cools and did not appear agitated or perturbed while the death sentence was pronounced.

Tombstone Justice Is Swift at the End of Rope; "Nice Looking Crowd" Attends Execution

(Epitaph, Nov. 18, 1900)

All that human agency and legal skill could do to save those whom the mandate of the law had marked for its own was done in behalf of Thomas Halderman and William Halderman, but Justice wept and would not be comforted. The blood of the two peace officers of Cochise county cried aloud and hushed the voice of mercy, **and at 12:40 o'clock these two young men forfeited their lives** to satisfy the ends of the law.

The importance of this case caused the bringing to bear upon those in power the strongest of influence both from those in high public station and private life. But the pardoning power was satisfied after a most thorough examination that the men had a fair and impartial trial; were defended by able attorneys and their conviction and sentence was legal. Twice the gallows, with its ghostly shadows flung across the prison windows, was in readiness and twice was the hand of mercy reached forth to give them a small respite from their impending fate.

The first respite was given when the appeal to the supreme court was taken, the next was granted by President McKinley, and lastly by Governor Murphy who fixed today as the time which was the last. If a feeling of sympathy was inclined to steal over the hearts of those who knew the boys, on account of their youth and their conduct in prison during the long months which they have awaited their doom, it was overshadowed by the cold blooded and cruel manner in which they dealt out death to their unsuspecting victims, for which they today paid the penalty.

Windows Lined

The time set for the execution was between the hours of 12 noon and 1 p.m. A large crowd was present, and anxiously waited the time when admittance would be had to the prison yard where the execution was to take place. All the court house windows on the second floor facing and overlooking the prison yard were lined with people to witness the execution. About 100 pertsons were in the prison yard.

When the iron door leading into the jail was swung open a solemn hush prevailed and all eyes turned in that direction. Shortly after the condemned men appeared. Thomas Halderman in the lead in charge of Deputy Sheriff Johnson, and William Halderman in charge of Deputy Sheriff Bravin. Sheriff Scott White and Rev. Elliott followed closely in the line down the narrow steps to the scaffold.

Thomas Halderman, the younger prisoner, had just emerged from the jail door and facing the crowd said, "Hello hombres," then placing his hand to his eyes to shield them from the sun's rays, said, "The sun's hot, ain't it?"

The prisoners walked to the scaffold and mounted the steps with a firm tread and exhibition of nerviness that was most surprising. They showed no sign of the least faltering and with rare courage and remarkable boldness advanced to the attendants in the final arrangements.

William Halderman stepped to the front under the dangling noose and surveyed the crowd below.

No Nervousness

"Nice looking crowd," he said with a wave of his hand. He even smiled and remarked, "Some of you fellers are shaking already."

Thomas Halderman, who was equally nervy, held the rope and looked over the crowd below. Turning to his brother he observed, "These people look all right." He looked at the noose and mechanically placed it over his own head. He then listened attentively to the reading of the death warrant by Sheriff Scott White.

Thomas paid marked attention throughout but the elder brother on the other hand paid no attention whatever and was the while engaged in conversation with Deputy Sheriff Brav in. At the conclusion of the reading Sheriff White asked if they wished to make a statement.

Thomas Halderman spoke up promptly and in a clear voice said, "I have nothing to say and guess it would not do any good anyway. I forgive you all and hope you will forgive me."

"This will be an experience that ought to benefit all of you," William Halderman said, "I hope I will meet you all. I pray for you and hope you will pray for me."

The straps were tied about the body and ankles. During this the prisoners noted some acquaintances below and made a few personal remarks or nodded to each. While standing on the trap door and firmly strapped, William Halderman, addressing Sheriff White, said, "Kindly give us time for a little prayer."

Rev. Elliott who had been constantly with them and afforded much religious consolation, stepped forward and after having the two condemned men clasp each other's hand, read a solemn prayer which was most impressive.

Final Salutations

The black caps were drawn over the heads of the prisoners and as it shut them out from the sight of the faces below, both men said in chorus, "Good bye, boys. Pray for us." Each again said goodbye and the crowd answered, "goodbye."

The trap was sprung at exactly 12:40 and Dr. H. F. Walter, county physician and Dr. Toney of Pearce were in attendance. At the end of 13 minutes Thomas Halderman was pronounced dead while the death of William Halderman was not announced until two minutes later. The bodies of the condemned men were taken to the cemetery this afternoon and the drama ends.

The Crime

The crime for which William and Thomas Halderman died today was the murdering of Teddy Moore, a boy of about 18 years, the son of Mart Moore, an old timer in the territory. The evidence adduced on the trial of the case showed that a warrant was placed in the hands of Constable Ainsworth of Pearce for the arrest of the Haldermans upon a charge of violating the livestock law; that Ainsworth appreciated that he was to arrest the Haldermans at the Wilson ranch or at a remote place in the Chiricahua mountains and got Teddy Moore to accompany him in making the arrests.

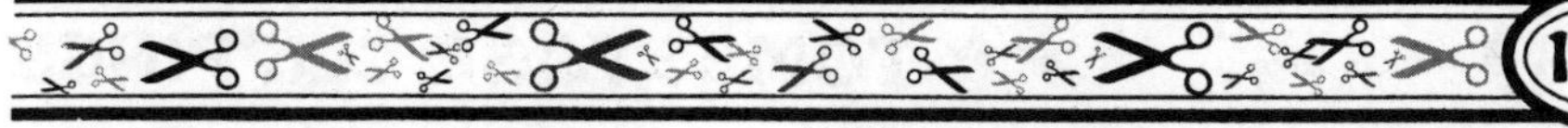

July 23, 1893

Arriving at the Wilson ranch-house, they called for the Haldermans to come out. The two appeared and Ainsworth told them he had warrants for their arrest, and would have to take them to Pearce. They agreed to go, and Ainsworth then asked if they had had breakfast yet, as it was early morning. They said they had not. Then he told them to get some and that he would wait.

The Haldermans later reappeared, one at each of the front doors with rifles, killing Ainsworth instantly and firing upon Teddy Moore who had wheeled his horse and started toward home. He died a few hours later from the effect of the last bullet fired at him, which had taken effect in his back. The Haldermans fled and were later captured in New Mexico.

TOMBSTONE PROSPECTOR

City and County Official Paper

PUBLISHED EVERY EVENING
(EXCEPT SUNDAY)
—BY—
S. C. BAGG, Editor and Proprietor.
OFFICE:
Fremont St., Opposite City Hall.

Entered in the Tombstone Postoffice as second class matter.

OFFICIAL DIRECTORY.

Mayor	Geo. Fitts
Chief of Police,	Hugh Pugh.
Councilmen:	
First Ward	Fred Fuss
Second Ward	Wm. Bartholomew
Third Ward	C. B. Tarbell
Fourth Ward	John Prinderville
COUNTY OFFICERS:	
Sheriff	Scott White
Treasurer	M. D. Scribner
Recorder	A. Wentworth
District Attorney	Wm C. Staehle
Probate Judge	W. D. Monmonier
Clerk District Court	A. H. Emanuel
Surveyor	H. G. Howe
Assessor	J. J. Patton
Court Commissioner	G. W. Swain

December 15, 1904

The Tombstone Prospector

WM. HATTICH, Editor and Proprietor.

Published at Tombstone, A. T., Every Day Except Sunday.

Telephone No. 1.

Subscription Rates:

One Year in Advance	$7 50
Six Months	$3 75
One Month	65c
Single Copies	5c
WEEKLY EPITAPH, Per Year	$3 00

Entered at the Postoffice in Tombstone as Second-Class Matter.

Our Watchword----"Cochise County First, the World Afterward."

TOMBSTONE, COCHISE COUNTY, ARIZONA—WEDNESDAY EVENING, JANUARY 20, 1904.

February 17, 1904

THE NEW TIME TABLE.

In Effect Jan. 12, 1904.

Leave Tombstone for Bisbee, Douglas, Naco, El Paso, 8 a. m.

Leave Tombstone for Benson, 10:15 a. m.

Leave Tombstone for Bisbee, Douglas, Naco, 1:55 p. m.

Leave Tombstone for Benson, 6:05 p. m.

Arrive from Benson and points east and west, 9:15 a. m.

Arrive from Bisbee, Douglas, Naco, 11:30 a. m.

Arrive from Benson, 3:15 p. m.

Arrive from El Paso and way points 7:35 p. m.

$1,000 REWARD.

The above reward will be paid for the arrest and detention in any jail in the United States or in the Republic of Mexico, of Albert Alvord and Wm. Stiles, who broke jail in Tombstone on the night of December 15, 1903.

The above reward will be paid for the arrest of both, or $500 for either man. The reward is good for one year. Wire at my expense.

A. V. LEWIS.
Sheriff of Cochise County.

Tombstone, Ariz., Jan. 2, 1904.

February 14, 1904

WORK ON THE HILL

Sinking Below the Water Level at Four Different Points

DISTRICT IS DRAINED

Drifting for Known Ore Bodies Hundred Feet Below the Old Water Level—Shipments of Ore

The Tombstone Consolidated Mines Company is now operating at four different shafts below the water level, and the fact that work is under way at widely separate points within the limits of the huge water basin that underlies the Tombstone district is a matter of considerable significance, in that the water problem is fast fading away and that each stubborn obstacle of the watery depths is being overcome and made to yield to the ingenuity of approved scientific engineering and modern mining methods which have characterized the operations of the company.

The four points above mentioned are the big main shaft of the company, the Emerald, the West Side and the Silver Thread. At the two latter places—which are some fifty feet below the old water level—some good ore is being extracted and shipped, while at the main shaft a drift is being run at the 700-level—100 feet below the water line—toward the phenomenal Contention and Grand Central ledges, to reach the rich ores that made these properties famous in the early days of the camp. This drift is in 120 feet.

At the Emerald, the incline shaft is now below the water line and will be crowded to the first station, when drifting will be started toward the ore zone.

When it is remembered that the distance between the Silver Thread on the north and the Emerald on the south is over a mile and a half, the magnitude of the work of the large pumping plant at the intermediate point in draining this immense district will be at once recognized. The mammoth pumps keep sending a swirling stream of nearly two million gallons daily to the surface, and the big four-compartment shaft is being continued downward to the 1000-foot level, which is the objective point of the company.

About three carloads of ore is being shipped daily by the company to the El Paso smelters, and about 100 tons per day is being shipped from the Lucky Cuss dumps to the same point. The latter dump contained some 12,000 to 15,000 tons of ore, which was contracted for by the smelter company.

January 14, 1904

Disastrous Runaway on Tombstone Streets

Considerable excitement was occasioned this morning by a runaway team that resulted disastrously. A team of horses attached to part of a Chinaman's vegetable wagon, came down Allen street in a wild race, and at the corner of Fourth and Allen the horses attempted to pass between a telephone pole and the sidewalk. Both horses made a sudden swerve to pass the pole, but the inside horse did not clear the obstruction and struck the big pole with such terrific force that he was instantly felled to the ground and was dead within a few minutes, his neck having been broken by the crash. The impact was heard for blocks, and the telephone pole was snapped in twain about seven feet from the top. The other horse was apparently uninjured and continued on toward Fairbank. The team and wagon belonged to a vegetable Chinaman. Before the horses arrived on Allen street the wagon bed had been lost in the runaway and at the time of the fatal collision with the telephone pole only the front wheels and running gear was in evidence

KILLING OF WILD HORSES

Cochise Range Gets Rid of Worthless Wild Equines

EXCITING INCIDENTS

March 2, 1904

The Extermination of Horses Going On All Over Range Section of the Territory

In the recent annual round-up of wild horses near Fredonia, Arizona, eighty animals were killed and seventeen were captured. Two parties of ranchmen engaged in the hunt, and, surrounding the herds drove them into a ravine, where the slaughter took place.

The wild horses were led by a fiery black stallion, which was game to the last. The best of the herd were roped and every effort was made to capture the stallion, but he made such a hard fight that it was found necessary to shoot him.

These horses increase so rapidly that every year the ranchmen find it necessary to exterminate them, and for this purpose annual round-ups are held. Several of these round-ups have been had in Cochise county, a recent wholesale killing of valueless range horses taking place on the Greene Cattle Company's ranges and along the San Pedro.

February 11, 1904

KILLED BY MEXICANS

Deputy Sheriff Meets Death While in Discharge of Duty

THREE ASSAILANTS

Dies from Injuries Received and Makes Dying Depostiion Charging Three Mexicans Prisoners Here.

Deputy Sheriff Arthur Wight was brought to Tombstone last evening from Black Diamond, where he had been mortally wounded by several Mexicans while in the discharge of his official duties. The unfortunate officer died about an hour after his arrival, and, although suffering great pain from a bullet wound that had shattered the bones of his leg and thigh, he met death heroicly and bravely.

From particulars had it is learned that a Mexican named Figueroa was arrested by Wight at Black Diamond for being drunk and disorderly and the offender placed in the local lock up. Shortly after three friends of the prisoner also intoxicated sought to release their companion and attempted to batter down the jail door. Wight re appeared on the scene and the three Mexicans intimated that they would kill him. and started for him, whereupon he hastened to his house to secure his Winchester. The three men shot at Wight as he emerged from his door, and, as the officer fell wounded, he fired one shot in the direction of his assailants, but without effect.

Wight was made as comfortable as possible and brought to Tombstone. Before leaving Black Diamond the wounded man, realizing that his end was near, made a deposition of the circumstances before Justice Monmonier and named his three Mexican assailants. Later Deputy Prewett arrested the three Mexicans They were brought to Tombstone this afternoon and landed behind the bars under a charge of murder.

Deputy Wight was a son of Alex. Wight of Pearce and was well and favorably known as an efficient officer.

Deceased was a member of Pearce Lodge, Knights of Pythias, and the funeral will take place under the auspices of that order, announcement of which will be made later.

February 12, 1904

FUNERAL OF OFFICER

Arthur Wright Buried Under Auspices of K. of P.

FORMER TOMBSTONITE

Had Served as Sheriff of Graham Co., and Known as a Good Officer —Leaves Wife and Family.

The funeral of Arthur Wight took place at 3 p. m. today from the undertaking parlors of C. Tarbell, the funeral being under the auspices of the K. of P. of which order deceased was an honored member. The funeral was well attended by friends who paying their last tribute of respect to the brave officer who met death at the hands of three Mexicans while in the discharge of his official duties. The deceased held positions of trust in Graham and Cochise counties, having served as sheriff of Graham county, being also elected to various official positions and was known as a brave and fearless officer. The deceased lived in Tombstone in the early days and is well known in Cochise county. He was son of Alexander Wight of Pearce, who is a Cochise county pioneer and represented this county in the 15th Territorial legislature. Deceased leaves a wife and three children and the sympathy of the community is extended the bereaved in their hour of loss.

February 12, 1904

TRIAL OF SOME CHINESE CASES

One Celestial Proves His Point and Permitted to Remain in the United States.

FIVE CHINESE IN TOMBSTONE JAIL.

Judge Doan arrived last evening from Florence to hold United States court in the hearing of Chinese cases. One Chinaman, named Yee Gee Chee, was released from custody after a trial of his case, it being shown that Chee was a native born Chinaman and had lost his papers. The cases against four other Chinamen, held for being illegally in the United States, were postponed until March 31. These Celestials were placed in the Tombstone jail awaiting trial.

February 11, 1904

TO ENLIST WITH THE JAPS

Rough Riders from the West Enter the Service of the Mikado.

SEEKING AMERICAN FIGHTERS.

Edward Thomas, son of Night-Watchman Thomas, of Bisbee and who is well known in Tombstone, and who served in the Spanish American war in the Phillipines, has received a letter from a companion in Texa who also served with him in the same company of rough riders has been organized in Texas, and all of their expenses have been paid and advanced, necessary to take them to Japan, and enter the service of the army of the Mikado as a "Rough Rider" regiment and that they are all ready to depart at once. There are a good many American youths who would be glad of the opportunity to enlist in the Japanese army.

March 3, 1904

MRS. STILES INTERVIEWED

Wife of Outlaw Tells of Experiences With Officers

TALKS OF HUSBAND

Came to Tombstone to See Alvord and Had a Brief Interview at Jail. Determined to Stay at Ranch

"I don't mind telling you that I came here to see Burt Alvord," said Mrs. William Stiles wife of the noted outlaw, to a PROSPECTOR reporter last evening.

Mrs. Stiles will easily tip the scales at 200 pounds and her countenance indicates a cheerful disposition. She has dark complexion and speaks Spanish and English fluently. She wears a breastpin bearing an excellent likeness of her outlaw husband, and referred to "Billy" in endearing terms.

"Alvord is wounded and sick, and as he sent for me, I called at the jail to see him for a few moments before he was taken to Yuma. I am sorry for him.

"No, I know of no proposition for Billy's surrender and I hope the officers will never get him. I feel very much worried about him, as he is not afraid and may be caught in some trap by the officers. I have not heard from him in a long time since the jail break and Rangers, deputies and officers galore are constantly about our tent; as if they expected to find Billy at home." And Mrs. Stiles laughed heartily.

"One thing I do not like," continued Mrs. Stiles, "is the way the Rangers have been breaking into our tent whenever they feel like it. They come in with Winchesters and guns and look under the beds and around the tent looking for Billy. It is a regular thing so I don't get alarmed any more and my sister and nephew are also getting used to it. But it is not right.

"I expect to live and stay at the ranch as long as I want to—if I have to eat roots to keep alive.

"I know nothing of the reported bullion robbery," said Mrs. Stiles. "If I had that eight thousand dollars I would build a house at my place and stay there."

March 2, 1904

SAW STILES IN MEXICO

Rancher Meets the Outlaw Below the Line

WILL NOT SURRENDER

Mrs. Stiles, Wife of the Fugitive, Visits Tombstone, but Is Silent As Regards Her Mission

Mrs. William Stiles, wife of the famous outlaw, was a Tombstone visitor today.

If Mrs. Stiles is here on any business connected with the rumored negotiations looking to the surrender of Stiles, she religiously adheres to a strict policy of secrecy and does not give out any information whatever on the subject.

Mrs. Stiles states she does not know the whereabouts of her husband and gives no information regarding him.

Joe Cobbs, a well-known rancher on the river, and who is located near the Stiles ranch, brought Mrs. Stiles here. He, likewise, is reticent as to the mission of the visitor. Mr. Cobbs, however, claims to have seen Stiles two days since some twenty or thirty miles below the line. He says that Stiles told him that he did not propose to be captured alive; that if the officers succeeded in catching him they would have to do it with bullets, and that, in the event of a battle, he would endeavor to make it interesting for the officers. Cobbs says Stiles did not appear to be wounded. He saw him but a few moments and the conversation was a brief one.

A social dance will be held at Gage Hall on Friday evening next and a pleasant time is assured to all who attend.

May 19, 1904

PEARL IN THE TOILS

Arizona's Female Ex-Bandit Gains More Notoriety.

A KANSAS ESCAPADE

Is Charged With Aiding Some Car Thieves—Tells Jail Officials of Her Arizona Experiences.

"Pearl Hart," also known as Mrs. I. P. Keele, the famous ex bandit, who lived in El Paso for a short while and who was here for a few days last summer en route to Kansas City after having been pardoned from the Arizona penitentiary is again in trouble

Pearl has been arrested at Kansas City, Kan., for complicity in receiving stolen goods and abetting a gang of pickpockets.

Mrs. Keele has confessed to Chief Murray of Kansas City, Kan., that she is the Pearl Hart who robbed the Arizona stage coach. At first she steadily denied it until Chief Murray finally told her he would have her picture taken and could find out her identity by sending it to Arizona. Then she confessed her identity, although she would not admit being implicated in any of the offenses of which she is suspected. She may be held in connection with the stealing of sugar from a Chicago Great Western freight car. She denies, however, that she received any of the stolen goods, although she admits having bought a sack of sugar and some canned goods from a young man who came to her sister's house. She said that he represented that he was selling flood goods.

Pearl was in a reminiscent mood when visited in the city jail at Kansas City, Kan. She told of her motive for robbing the stage coach and also related a number of romantic tales of bandit life in the far west.—El Paso News.

May 19, 1904

MET DEATH ON THE RAIL

Cochise County Resident Who is Killed Under Mysterious Circumstances.

GROUND TO DEATH UNDER WHEELS

J. B. Parks of Wilcox who is visiting in Douglas, tells of a man losing his life in Wilcox by being run over by a train, his body being found Friday night about 10 o clock near the water tank. Mr. Parks could not remember the name, but knows that it was a German name. On the deceased was found a gold watch and more than $70 in money. The man was well dressed and among his papers was found a saloon license authorizing him to do business in Douglas; also among his papers was found some certificates of stock in a California water company. The coroner's jury rendered a verdict that the deceased met his death in an unknown manner. There was a suspicion among some of the people in Wilcox that the man had been carried to the place where he was found after his death. The train had ground all the flesh off his left leg and passed over his chest and left shoulder. Still where he was found on the track but little blood was to be seen.

May 19, 1904

Soldiers In Tombstone Enroute to Huachuca

Lieutenant Myers, in command of 75 members of the 6th Cavalry, arrived in Tombstone today from Ft. Grant en route to Ft. Huachuca. The lieutenant and command will remain over night and continue on to their destination tomorrow. The camping ground of the soldiers is at the depot and is quite a point of interest for a large number of townspeople who want to see how Uncle Sam's soldiers fare while out on a march.

Who Is He?

The unfortunate man spoken of in yesterday's Epitaph as having been found in a vacant house on Wednesday night, and upon being taken to the hospital, where he died, was buried this morning and his identity buried with him. Hundreds of people went to look at him as he lay in the undertaking rooms of Watt & Tarbell, but although many recognized his features as being familiar his name or occupation was a mystery that remained unsolved. He was between forty-five and fifty years of age, about six feet high, dark hair and whiskers, Roman Nose, grey eyes, clean-cut features, long finger nails, and evidently a man of intelligence. His body was clothed with a red undershirt, gray overshirt, canton flannel drawers and a pair of blue, riveted overalls. The latter were soiled with grease in front indicating that he probably had been an engineer or employed in some similar capacity. He came up from Fairbank with Durward's freight wagon six days ago. He no doubt died from pneumonia, and never uttered a word during his stay at the hospital, being too far gone when found to utter a sound. He carried a valise and a bundle of blankets, but no papers by which he might be identified.

June 10, 1904.

A justice of peace in a remote precinct in Cochise county was recently requested by the attorney for a local goat thief, to "charge the jury." He had never presided in a case before, and turning to the jury remarked, "Come to think it over gentlemen, it is my duty to charge you in this case. Now since this is the first time you were ever up before me I will only charge you a dollar apiece." The jury considered that they got off light.

For All Ailments!

DR. LOUIE'S EXTRACT OF MAMMOTH TOOTH

This famous remedy is carefully prepared on the high bank of el Rio de San Pedro from the freshest ingredients available. Noted for its miraculous powers and the many cures effected, it is handled exclusively by—

The European Medical Staff and Special Surgeons and Physicians of the Liebig World Dispensary and International Surgical Institute, 400 Geary street, San Francisco, Cal.

At Occidental Hotel

FIGHTING WHISKY

July 10, 1904.

Last night something happened on Allen street, yea in the middle thereof. For a few minutes the monotony was relieved. The shipping clerk had evidently made a mistake and billed in a demijohn of scrapping whisky. After two bibulations thereof, two powerful gentry went into the middle of the street without referee or seconds. In a three round bout one was knocked out, and as the one he attempted to smother a big lump was raised on the eye of the other, and while they rejoiced in the absence of Bravin, they needed the surgical science of Sabin. In other words, their faces would have made a tempting sign for a raw hamburger shop. That demijohn was corked, sealed and delivered to be exported, and no more trouble is expected.

CHINATOWN CONFLAGRATION.

February 21, 1904.

Last night about nine-thirty o'-clock an exploded lamp caused a blaze at a Chinese house on Third street, which burned a table and Chinese ornaments before the same was extinguished. The entire Chinese population were considerably agitated and it was many hours before the Celestials and babel of voices were sufficiently calmed to permit of ordinary conversation. When three of four Chinks address each other simultaneously and "tell how it happened" there is a noise "like unto the voices of many winds."

UNDERTAKING PARLORS OF

C. B. Tarbell

New Hearse, New Goods, Everything New.

Coffins, Caskets, Robes, Etc.

From the Plainest to the Finest Made.

Th Columbia Iron Caskets kept constantly in Stock.

Bodtes Temporarily or Permcnently Embalmed by the latesi process.

☞Night orders left at Hare & Page's livery office promptly attended to.

Drugs, Medicines.

PRESCRIPTIONS CAREFULLY compounded, day or night. Stock first-class and being contiually replenished with everything the town demands such as

Pure Drugs, Patent Medicines, Toilet Articles, Perfumes etc

Too numerous to mention. Orders from the surrounding country promptly attended to. Patronage respectfully solicited. Prices reasonable.

H. F. WILLIAMS.

West side of Fifth st. opposite Express Office, Tombstone, Ariz.

November 2, 1880

MELROSE RESTAURANT,

FREMONT STREET, BETWEEN FOURTH AND FIFTH,

Tombstone, Arizona.

Mrs. M. L. Woods,

Proprietress.

The Largest and Most Elegantly Furnished Dining Hall in the City. Careful and prompt attention to guests. Special provision made for private dining parties.

REGULAR BOARDING, $8 A WEEK. SINGLE MEALS, 50C

November 2, 1880

EAGLE MARKET,

TRIBOLET BROS., PROPRIETORS.

ALLEN STREET, COR. FOURTH, OPPOSITE COSMOLITAN HOTEL

BEEF, PORK, MUTTON AND SALT MEATS,

Sausages of all kinds, both Domestic and Imported, a Specialty. Meats delivered in all parts of the city free of charge.

G. TRIBOLET, MANAGER.

SONOMA WINE AT MILEY'S WINE HOUSE,

[illegible]

[illegible] prices.

[illegible] Sherry and [illegible] Wines

THE RED STORE.

Staple and Fancy

GROCERIES,

Fine TEAS and COFFEES a Specialty.

Wines and Liquors.

R. P. MANSFIELD

Fifth Street. - - Tombstone, A. T.

March 17, 1904.

Floto's Circus, a large tented aggregation traveling with their own special trains, have included Tombstone in their western tour and will be here on April fourth, advance announcement to that effect having been received here. The city will doubtless be covered with mammoth circus posters shortly, and the small boy will await the date with great anxiety.

CONFIRMS STORY.

February 14, 1904.

John Tener, the man who was held up by Alvord and Stiles was in Douglas to-day and said that it is a positive fact that they were the men who robbed him of eight thousand dollars bullion. He confirms the report that the outlaws passed through Nacozari within the last three days.

THE
COMET

Frank Payla, Prop.

Opposite Ice House.

Card and
Sample Rooms

Wines, Liquors
and Cigars

THE ARIZONA CLUB.

AL BONNER, Props.

Wines, Liquors
and Cigars.

"The Best, and
Only the Best
is our Motto."

Allen Street, Near Fifth.

KING'S
SALOON

Choice Line of Wines
and Cigars. Imported and Domestic Cigars.

Allen Street, Bet. 3rd & 4th.

CITY
BARBER
SHOP
AND BATH
ROOMS.

B. Miano,
Prop.

Newly renovated and repaired inside and out.
Large Bath Rooms and First-Class Tubs.
Shaving, Shampooing, Hair Cutting
Years of practice and Experience.

THE
ARCADIA
SALOON.

JAS. HAGAN, Prop

Choicest Wines, Liquors and Cigars. Every attention and courtesy shown to patrons.

NEXT DOOR TO CAN CAN.

Pony Saloon.

J. H. Marrs, Prop.

Finest Stock of Wines, Liquors and Cigars in the Territory.

Private Club Rooms Attached.

Best and Purest Brands of All Whiskies, Brandies, Wines,

Allen Street, Between 4th and 5th Sts.

Butter. Fresh Fruit

Wanted! Every Man, Woman and Child in Tombstone to know that we give the BEST VALUE for the LEAST money

Sneed Brothers. Phone 64. Allen Street

Notions. Sweet Cream.

Diavolo, The Prince of Dare-Devils, "Loops the Loop"

On a Bicycle with the Loop Open at the Top Jumping Head Downward a Distance of Fifteen feet.

February 5, 1903

PERRY WILDMAN & CO.

THE LEADING GROCERS.

Buying in car load lo:s we - ready to meet all competition. It will pay you to get our prices before buying elsewhere.

Our Stock is Always New and Fresa.

We Make a Specialtv ot Wines and Liquors for Familv and Kedic alUse

WE KEEP ONLY THE BEST.

Phone No. 12 Allen St. Bet. 4th and 5

February 5, 1903

Do You Use Perfume?

IF SO, WHY NOT USE THE BEST?

We have just received a large line of Roger & Gillet's Fine Perfumes, Toilet Articles, Etc.

TOMBSTONE DRUG CO. Ed R. Flach, Prop.

FIFTH ST., OPPOSITE W. F. CO

Prospector
February 5, 1903

SUITS MADE TO ORDER

SHOES FOR MEN AND BOYS

Are you "Sore" on Low Shoes? No heel rubbing in our kind. They fit and give comfort. They hold shape and wear as well as though you had paid more.

Our Stronghold is Quality.

Our goods have not been moving around on the shelves for the last ten or fifteen years. Only once, from the factory to our store, Always the best at the price.

JOHN ROCK,

XCLUSIVE MEN'S OUTFITTER. Allen bet. 4th [illegible]

SUITS MADE TO ORDER

GYPSY BAND ON MOVE.

December 4, 1904.

About a dozen gypsy maidens fluttered into town this morning. The reporter happened to be ambling aimlessly and innocently, when he was overtaken by a phalanx of red calico and other things. The reporter did not want his fortune told as he knew he was strictly up against it in the near future and did not want to walk the plank of adversity till his time came, so he made a dive into King's blacksmith shop, crawled under the bellows and escaped. The oriental females then chattered away at every pedestrian who happened along, like so many magpies, till Chief Bravin came along and advised them that it would cost them ten dollars a day to tell fortunes in Tombstone, and they were soon on the wing. George understands these people, who are defined in Webster as "One of a vagabond race, whose tribes coming originally from India, entered Europe in the fourteenth or fifteenth century and are now scattered over Turkey, Russia, Spain, Hungary, England, etc., living by theft, fortune telling, horse jockeying, tinkering and the like."

CASE OF FRIENDSHIP.

A Cochise County Man Relieved of His Sentence in Yuma.

February 5, 1910.

The Yuma Sentinel has the following story which is of interest to Cochise county readers, as the occurence is laid in this county:–

Jose Cruz was paroled out of the penitentiary the latter part of last week. Jose was sent up from Cochise county in eighteen ninety-six to serve ten years for murderous assault. It appears that during a revel somewhere down in Cochise county Joe and another man had trouble and the latter was almost killed during the fight. Joe silently slid out for Mexico and in the course of time a friend was arrested, tried, convicted and sentenced to ten years at Yuma. The guilty party was safe in Mexico, no one even suspecting Joe. However, he heard of his friend's conviction and he left his safe retreat to hurry back to the United States where he gave himself up, told his story, pleaded guilty and took the ten years from his friend.

Joe is an excellent man and his incarceration has not hardened his character. During his perio of imprisonment he never associated with the other prisoners being always found by himself, and his sacrifice for his friend stamps him a noble hearted fellow."

Prospector
February 4, 1890

The funeral of the late Alfred Richards was largely attended this afternoon by the friends of the deceased. The Tombstone band lead the solemn procession as it wended its way to the cemetery. The occasion was one of more than an ordinary nature. The manner in which the deceased met his death and his sudden separation from his friends created a feeling in the breasts of those who even had not known him personally, that they were interested in seeing the being who had caused his untimely taking off, speedily pay the penalty for his awful crime.

February 4, 1890

The deputy and posse who were in pursuit of the murderers of David Duncan, have returned to Tombstone after a fruitless run. They followed the trail for four days but lost it and could not find it again. They came upon the dead carcass of a cow that had been killed and partially skinned. The Mexicans had cut out a few ribs from the choicest part and cooked them and gone on. The cow was of the snake brand. The murder adds another to the mysteries that will probably never be cleared up.

Proved To Be A Desperado

July 6, 1907

After several months, during which a thorough investigation has been made, it has been finally proved beyond a doubt that J.A. Tracy, who was shot and killed by Capt. Harry Wheeler of the Arizona Rangers, who was at that time lieutenant of the company, was a desperado with a record of two men killed, and a price of $500 on his head, dead or alive. Captain Wheeler refused the reward tendered him by the board of supervisors of a Nevada county; requesting that the reward be paid to the widow of one of Tracy's victims.

PREHISTORIC RUINS.

While Making Excavation For Reservoir Workmen Uncover Old Pottery And Human Bones.

SIMILAR TO RUINS AT COCHISE STRONGHOLD.

January 22, 1914

What are thought to be prehistoric ruins have been uncovered in Cochise county according to reports reaching here yesterday. It appears that while several men were making excavations for a reservoir three miles from the Perrin land grant on the Barbacomari, they unearthed numerous pieces of ancient pottery, in addition to human skulls and bones. A further search of the diggings is now in progress, with the hopes of ascertaining the extent of the ruins. Some years ago the skeliton of a horse and man were found near this place, the skeles of both being intact and in good condition, and had evidently been buried several hundred years ago, while numerous other finds of a similar character have been made in that vicinity at different intervals. Prehistoric ruins were also recently found in the vicinity of the Cochise Stronghold, near Tombstone in the Dragoon mountains, and it is understood that examinations of the same are about to be made by the Smithsonian Institute at Washington. It is being rumored that the Perrin land grant, the second largest land grant in Arizona, is to be put under cultivation by its and that they will in the near future give their entire time to agriculture and stockraising. The grant is owned and controlled by the Perrin Brothers of Williams.

Virgil Earp has been working a claim near Thumb Butte, from which he has been taking ore which assays sixty ounces in silver and thirty per cent lead. He has also a promising gold claim, which he is working – Journal Miner.

Epitaph
July 24, 1910

Show and Dance Postponed Until Tonight

The amusement lovers of Tombstone were sadly disappointed last evening on account of the severe electrical storm, which played havoc with the the electric light wires around the city and broke down the wires connecting the current into Schieffelin opera house, and for this reason the excellent opening bill had to be postponed until 8 o'clock tonight. Many, regardless of the pouring down rain, went to the opera house last night only to hear the disappointing news of the postponement of the show.

About thirty dance lovers gathered at the Gage hall and danced to the sweet strains of music from the famous Venne's Orchestra until 10 o'clock, when Manager Miller announced its postponement until after the show tonight. The music was sweet and no doubt a big crowd will greet musicians at the Gage Hall tonight, as well as at the show in Schieffelin. Remember to "meet me at the show 8 o'clock this evening."

Governor's Proclamation.

Executive Department
Territory of Arizona,
Office of the Governor.

To all to Whom these Presents may Come, Greeting:

Whereas, I am informed that William C. Drake, late private, Troop G., Fourth Cavalry was found murpered at Sulphur, Springs, south of Wilcox, Arizona, on the 29th day of September last, and no trace of the murderer or murderers has been discovered,

Now, therefor, I, C. Meyer Zulick Governor of the Territory of Arizona, by virtue of the authority in me vested, do hereby offer and proclaims a reward of five hundred dollars for the arrest and conviction of the murderer or murderers of the said William C. Drak .

In witness hereof, I have set my hand and caused the Great Seal of [SEAL] the Territory to be affixed thereto.

Done at Prescott, the Capital, the 26th day of November, A. D., 1887.

C MEYER ZULICK.

By the Governor:
J. A. BAYARD,
Secretary of the Territory.

Warning Notice.

All parties are hereby warned that the first northern extension of the Mamie mine, known as the combination mine, is exclusively owned by me and is not subject to sale or use by any other save myself. JACK MARTIN.

—$250 Reward—

(Epitaph, Jan. 31, 1887)

The Sheriff of the County of Cochise is hereby authorized to offer a reward for the arrest and conviction of the party or parties who attempted to kill J. S. Clark and wife on the evening of January 4th, 1887.

(signed) John H. Slaughter
Sheriff

Grand Raffle.

May 10, 1887.

The horse and buggy, extra buggy pole, gents riding saddle offered for sale at the O.K. Corral, will be raffled off as soon as all the tickets are sold. All of the above can be seen at the O.K. Corral. Tickets on sale in the leading business houses of this city.

Asks Governor To Protect "Road Runner"

June 15, 1912

Herbert Brown, clerk of the superior court and curator of the university museum, constitutes himself a defender of the remarkable bird known as the Arizona "road runner" in a letter which he has written to Governor Hunt, asking that the "road runners" be spared an untimely death.

"I learn, much to my surprise and regret," he states, "that the proposed new game laws contains which will ultimately lead to the destruction of the road-runner, one of the most entertaining and interesting of our western birds.

"Of all Arizona birds it is most typical. Without it, something would be missing on an Arizona landscape. Its food consists of mice, snakes, lizards, crabs, snails, grasshoppers, centipedes, caterpillars, beetles and cactus fruit. I have heard, read and seen many things in its favor, and never read or before heard one word of its disparagement."

The letter continues with many quotations from the works of ornithologists concerning the road-runner, and closes with a plea for its preservation.

$400 REWARD.

The above named reward will be paid by Troop G, 4th U. S. Cavalry, Fort Bowie, Arizona, for the apprehension and conviction of the murderer of William C. Drake, (late private of said troop) at Sulphur Springs, Arizona, on the 29th of September.

GEO. WILLIAMS,
Sergeant

The O.K. Corral

Shown as it appeared about the time the Railroad came to Tombstone

Funeral Of John Behan, A Cochise Pioneer

June 15, 1912

The funeral of John Behan took place at Tucson Saturday, many Cochise pioneers paying a last tribute of respect by attending the funeral of the deceased. Behan first came to Arizona in 1863 and served as sheriff of Yavapai county and later saw him in like position in Cochise county. He also was superintendent of the penitentiary and was a vereran of the Spanish-American war, seeing service in the Cuban campaign.

In 1879 he came to Cochise county and became this county's first sheriff, an office which at that time was combined with tax collector and assessor. He was appointed by Governor Fremont. As sheriff he rendered conspicuous service against the bands of Mexican and American bandits who had rendered life dangerous and rather unprofitable along the Mexican border, and took an active part in suppressing the cattle war which was an outgrowth of the Wyatt Earp feud in Tombstone.

The death of Behan marks the passing of another Arizona pioneer, who helped make history, and his demise causes a pang of deep regret among the many friends who knew him.

CURLEY BILL.

Mystery Lingers On As To Bill's End.

This Robin Hood of the Tombstone area accidentally killed Marshal White, Tombstone's first marshal, made a fortune from cattle "shot-gunned" across the border to evade paying duty at the International Line and by hijacking robbers and highwaymen, then disappeared.

Wyatt Earp claimed to have shot him in French Joe Canyon in the Whetstone mountains. Doc Holliday was accused of shooting him from his horse at Robber's Roost and a cowboy wearing clothes like Curley's and riding his horse was buried in Boothill.

The Benson postmaster claimed he loaned him a horse to ride to Wyoming and a new start.

The Epitaph offered a $1,000 reward for proof that Curley was alive. The Tombstone Prospector offered $1,000 for proof Curley was dead. Neither sum was ever claimed.

In 1920, Avery Curry, one of Charleston's first business men, claimed he had just returned from Chihuahua, Mexico, where he visited the former outlaw on his prosperous ranch.

July 1882

Editor's Note:

"Wyatt Earp killed 'Curly Bill' Brocius at Mescal Springs, wounding Johnny Barnes at the same time. On his death bed, Barnes told Fred Dodge that Wyatt killed 'Curly Bill' and that his 'Cowboy' friends secretly buried the body on Frank Patterson's ranch. Barnes also admitted that he was the one who shot and crippled Virgil Earp."

March 3, 1904

DEATH OF SCHACKMAN

Arizonian With Romantic History Dies in Tombstone

A FRUITLESS SEARCH

Was After the Lost Dutchman Mine and Kept Diary of His Experience Believed it in Cochis County

Charles T. Schackman, a pioneer prospector and miner, died at the County Hospital today of Bright's disease. Schackman spent many years in Arizona in a fruitless search for the Lost Dutchman mine of which he claimed to have had information, having personally known the original discoverer. He never lost faith or confidence in the re-discovery of the famous property, and spent years in the hills on his chase of the will-o' the wisp, only coming to town to earn money enough for another grub stake. He spoke very little of his mission, preferring to keep his own counsel and continue his search alone. Schackman doubtless believed that the Lost Dutchman was in Cochise county, as he had been prospecting in the various mountain ranges within the county up to the time of his illness. He was well known in Tombstone and throughout Southern Arizona.

Among the effects left by Schackman was a diary of his trips in search of the Lost Dutchman, the record kept extending over a period of two years.

Deceased left no relatives in Arizona, so far as is known, but is believed to have a brother in New York, who has been notified.

HOLIDAY PRESENTS!

HOLIDAY PRESENTS.

Just Received at the

Pioneer Jewelry Store,

The Finest, Largest and Best Selected Stock of

JEWELRY, DIAMONDS, WATCHES, CHAINS

Gold and Silver Filigree Goods in Latest Designs,

SILVERWARE and HOLIDAY NOVELTIES

Ever Brought to this Territory.

Prices Reduced to Suit the Times. Call and be Convinced.

H. SCHMIEDING, Prop.

HOLIDAY PRESENTS.

HOLIDAY PRESENTS!

THE RUSS HOUSE!

MISS NELLIE CASHMAN, Manager.

Thoroughly Refitted. Everything New

Eastern Waiters. White Cooks.

MEALS 25 CENTS AND UPWARDS

Board $6.00 per Week, in Advance. $6.50, if Paid Monthly.

June 3, 1909.

It happened in The Epitaph office: Two winsome young ladies called to liquidate a small account. The amount was handed over when the payee was asked if she wanted a Bill. Blushes enveloped her dimpled cheek and quickly but gently she replied "NO!" And yet some people wonder why some men remain bachelors!

WOMAN SUFFRAGE BILL.

February 21, 1909.

Councilman Ben Goodrich of Cochise county to-day presented a bill in the council to grant suffrage to women. The measure provides that women shall be allowed to vote at all elections. No comment was made on the bill when it was introduced. It is not probable that it will be passed.

EDITORIAL.

TOMBSTONE'S SEMI-CENTENNIAL.

June 27, 1929

Tombstone is discussing a proposal to formally celebrate the semi-centennial of its founding. Fifty years is no great age for a city to have attained, and compared with Tucson the county capital of Cochise has no more than reached the gosling age, but in terms of change it might have been founded five hundred years ago. It lives in the mellow light of romance, not only for its dwellers but for its wandering sons. These were formerly so many, so adventurous, and so widespread that each week Bill Hattich was enable to announce some sensational feat accomplished by a "former Tombstoner." Every Telegraphed news story telling of an unusual accomplishment–from the climbing of a porch to the climbing of a hitherto unscaled precipice–was susceptible of localization, for all adventurers it was suspected, must at some time have tarried at Tombstone. Thus "old Tombstoners" each week brought to Editor and Publisher Bill Hattich rich cargo of sensation and amazement, the news media of the wide world poured a steady stream of grist into the Epitaph's hopper.

Tucson and Tombstone are closely linked in history and Cochise capital may count on the sympathetic patronage of Old Pueblo if it determines to celebrate its seimcentennial.–Tucson Citizen.

January 4, 1881

THE NEW TIME TABLE

In Effect July 17, 1904.

Leave Tombstone for Bisbee, Douglas, Naco, El Paso, 7:35 a m.

Leave Tombstone for Benson, 10:20 a. m.

Leave Tombstone for Bisbee, Dougas, Naco, 3:00 p. m.

Leave Tombstone for Benson, 6:45 p. m.

Arrive from Benson and points east and west, 8:45 a. m.

Arrive from Bisbee, Douglas, Naco 11:40 a. m.

Arrive from Benson, 4:10 p. m.

Arrive from El Paso and way point 8:20 p. m.

Time-Card Arizona & Colorado R. R

Leave Cochise for Pearce 11 a. m and 2:50 p. m.

Leave Pearce for Cochise 9 a. m and 1 p. m.

Connections at Cochise with the S P. R. R.

Effective July 1, 1903.

E. A. McFarland,
Asst. Gen. Manager, Naco, Ariz.

June 23 1893.

From an exchange, in an article speaking of the strangeness of newspaper names, the Prospector makes the following interesting excerpt: "Curious, also, is the conjunction of names which obtains in Tombstone, Arizona. The leading paper is the Epitaph, which is edited by an Englishman named Coffin and published by a man named Sexton. The publisher declines advertisements of undertakers, but appropriately inserts death notices gratis."

HELLDORADO.

Celebration Sidelights On What Is Being Done.

July 18, 1929

The fifieth anniversary Helldorado celebration will be strictly a home show, according to announcement by Mayor Krebs. Foreign concessions will not be allowed. In other words all concessions must conform to the spirit of the times. The council will issue licenses only to those that will assist in carrying out the general plan.

The old days will be brought back for all visitors who attend. One idea is considered with favor is to have the parade start from Boot Hill, portraying the return of long departed citizens to the old mining camp made ready to receive them. They will, of course, be welcomed by the host of old timers here in the flesh.

Several ideas for housing the visitors are being worked out. Among the plans discussed at the mass meeting were those of opening all homes by preparing the extra rooms for lodgings, renting tents and cots for a municipal tent city, opening additional camp grounds and procuring surplus army equipment. The housing committee may adopt a combination of these plans.

A.H. Gardner reminded those who attend the meeting about Tombstone, and the fifth will be off the press before the year is over. These are in addition to innumerable short stories, magazine articles, and references to the fifty-year-old mining town found in other books of the west.

Sheriff George R. Henshaw stated that he was not thoroughly convinced of the success of Helldorado at first, but after being questioned by many old timers regarding plans and the progress made, he knows the pioneers are very much interested. After all, it is their show and if they are in favor of the idea, which has been proved to be the fact, it cannot help being a great success.

It is difficult, in fact almost impossible to regard the whiskergrowning contract without a smile, but all citizens who have signed it and who consequently forsake the razor for three months will be helping to insure the success of the celebration. Beards of every shade and hue should be distinctive items of the msaculine costumes. Mayor Krebs has announced that he will call on every man in town to secure signatures.

It was brought out at the mass meeting that every old time and "days of '49" show held in Arizona in recent years has been studied with a view of incorporating the best features in Helldorado. It is a problem of what to leave out as much as what to include according to the city council.

"We will stand for no bootleggers," Mayor Krebs announced, in referring to the Helldorado celebration. "The show will be clean, and the city council will do everything in its power to broadcast the word that no boot-leggers will be tolerated."

(1910)

GRAND

SOCIAL DANCE

Gage Hall

To-Night, July 23rd

After the Show

Music by the Famous Phoenix Indian School Orchestra

Everybody is Welcome

Admission - - $1.00

GEM SALOON,

Allen St., bet. Fifth and Sixth.

THOMAS HARRIS, Prop.

The finest brands of cigars, and none but choice liquors and wines sold at this house. Also one of the finest

Billiard Tables in Town.

Fate of Tombstone Believed Sealed

July 8, 1930

TOMBSTONE, Ariz.—Grizzled pioneers walked the arcaded sidewalks of this desert town today, sadly shaking their heads. Tombstone—the "rip-roaringest town the west ever knew"—is disintegrating.

Until recently, this western community was the seat of government of Cochise county. In an election, Bisbee, a mining city, usurped that honor.

But the successors to Ed Schieffein, the Earps, Clantons and others who settled here unafraid of the murderous Apache Indian tribes that roamed and pillaged the southwest of half a century ago, donned their metaphorical guns and went into action. They appealed to the Arizona supreme court, claiming the election irregular.

And by the court decision, handed down late yesterday, Tombstone had lost its last honor. The county seat is to be moved to Bisbee. Already the citizens of the latter city have started work on a new court house.

Created by a freak of fate, Tombstone's history records some of the most dramatic incidents of the life of the far west. At one time its population reached 15,000 and it was the largest city between El Paso, Texas, and the Pacific coast. When the silver ore gave out, the "hell-roaring" mining camp inhabitants drifted away, until today barely 800 persons make their home here.

A goodly portion of the citizens who gathered on the board walks today predict Tombstone is doomed and that soon it will be one of the numerous ghost towns which dot the west.

But the more enthusiastic point out that Tombstone still has its Can-Can restaurant, the OK corral where the Earps and the Clantons shot it out, and the Bird Cage theater, where Eddie Foy and Lottie Crabtree entertained years back to the strains of a tin-pan piano.

In desperate gesture, these historic places will once more be thrown open to throngs during "Helldorado Days" next October, when Tombstone of Ed Schieffelin's days will function with theatrical perfection.

The Schieffelin

MOVING PICTURES
ILLUSTRATED SONGS

GRAND OPENING To-Night July 23, 1910

MUSIC BY THE FAMOUS VENNE ORCHESTRA

SHOW STARTS 8:00 PROMPTLY

Admission - - - 20 Cts
Children - - - - 10 Cts

ALHAMBRA SALOON.

TOMBSTONE, ARIZONA.

MELLGREN & NICHOLS, Proprietors

Finest Bar in the City.

OPEN DAY AND NIGHT

CHOICEST LIQUORS & CIGARS.

Checks, Drafts, Gold, "Adobes," and the larger the amounts the better, will be received daily: that is, I would like to receive them.

February 2, 1882

DAILY EPITAPH

Thursday Morning........Feb. 2, 1882

DRAW YOUR OWN INFERENCE.

Resignation of Virgil W. and Wyatt S. Earp as Deputy Marshals.

Below will be found the resignation of Virgil and Wyatt Earp, as deputy United States marshals. The document is a manly and generous one, and should meet with impartial criticism from the public. The position of deputy marshal on the frontier is no sinecure. An officer who honestly tries to do his duty encounters many perils that the public know not of, and raises within the breasts of criminals that desire for their death that comes from fear of the gallows and imprisonment. It would be as much out of place for a public journal, under the attendant circumstances, to endeavor to create public opinion upon these resignations, as to prejudge a case at court. It is sufficient that the matter is before the United States marshal, who has had ample opportunity to investigate the condition of affairs, and who will give the subject that deliberate and careful consideration that comes of experience in official life. The following is a copy of the resignation tendered:

TOMBSTONE, February 1, 1882.

Major C. P. Dake, United States Marshal, Grand Hotel, Tombstone—Dear Sir: In exercising our official functions as deputy United States marshals in this territory, we have endeavored always unflinchingly to perform the duties intrusted to us. These duties have been exacting and perilous in their character, having to be performed in a community where turbulence and violence could at almost any moment be organized to thwart and resist the enforcement of the processes of the court issued to bring criminals to justice. And while we have a deep sense of obligation to many of the citizens for their hearty co-operation in aiding us to suppress lawlessness, and their faith in our honesty of purpose, we realize that, notwithstanding our best efforts and judgment in everything which we have been required to perform, there has arisen so much harsh criticism in relation to our operations, and such a persistent effort having been made to misrepresent and misinterpret our acts, we are led to the conclusion that, in order to convince the public that it is our sincere purpose to promote the public welfare, independent of any personal emolument or advantages to ourselves, it is our duty to place our resignations as deputy United States marshals in your hands, which we now do, thanking you for your continued courtesy and confidence in our integrity, and shall remain subject to your orders in the performance of any duties which may be assigned to us, only until our successors are appointed.

Very respectfully yours,

VIRGIL W. EARP,
WYATT S. EARP.

WATT & TARBELL
Undertakers.

NO. 418 ALLEN STREET.
Next door to Hare & Page's
Livery Stable.

Undertaking and embalming in all its branches.

Orders filled on short notice from any part of the County. Night orders can be left at Hare & Page's Livery Stable

Preparing and removing bodies promptly attended to.

THE ALARM GIVEN

The moment the word of the shooting reached the Vizina and Tough Nut mines the whistles blew a shrill signal, and the miners came to the surface, armed themselves, and poured into the town like an invading army. A few moments served to bring out all the better portions of our citizens, thoroughly armed and ready for any emergency. Precautions were immediately taken to preserve law and order, even if they had to fight for it. A guard of ten men were stationed around the county jail, and extra policemen put on for the night.

EARP BROTHERS JUSTIFIED

The feeling among the best class of our citizens is that the Marshal was entirely justified in his efforts to disarm these men, and that being fired upon they had to defend themselves, which they did most bravely. So long as our peace officers make effort to preserve the peace and put down highway robbery—which the Earp brothers have done, having engaged in the pursuit and capture, where captures have been made, of every gang of stage robbers in the country—they will have the support of all good citizens. If the present lesson is not sufficient to teach the cow-boy element that they cannot come into the streets of Tombstone, in broad daylight, armed with six-shooters and Henry rifles to hunt down their victims, then the citizens will most assuredly take such steps to preserve the peace as will be forever a bar to further raids.

March 30, 1885

Tombstone Epitaph,

The Paper 'Too Tough To Die'

Following Ed Schieffelin's silver strike, Tombstone sprang from the desert floor, bringing pioneer printers and their presses.

In 1879, THE DAILY NUGGET became Tombstone's first newspaper. John Clum published the first DAILY EPITAPH on May 1, 1880 and THE EPITAPH and NUGGET became instant rivals (the victor you're reading now).

Through the 1880's and '90's, Tombstone saw many papers: THE TOMBSTONE, DAILY DEMOCRAT, AMERICAN, REPUBLICAN, VALLEY HERALD, TOMBSTONE DAILY PROSPECTOR, plus THE COCHISE DAILY RECORD which merged with the EPITAPH in the mid '80's.

THE DAILY EPITAPH and PROSPECTOR combined in the '90's to form the morning and evening papers. Later THE EPITAPH went weekly on Sundays while the PROSPECTOR continued as an evening daily, and birth was given to THE ARIZONA KICKER, a weekly.

THE DAILY PROSPECTOR suspended publication on February 29, 1924, and in 1928 THE BORDERLAND TIMES was consolidated to form today's TOMBSTONE EPITAPH.

About the Editor

The first Traywick to arrive in America was John, who landed in Charleston, South Carolina in 1662. He had two sons, John and James, the former eventually settling in Tennessee and the latter in Alabama.

Ben T. Traywick, a descendent of John Traywick, was born in Watertown, Tennessee on August 3, 1927.

James Joseph Wiggins, Ben's maternal great-grandfather, was a private in the Confederate Army, Company B, 16th Tennessee Infantry Regiment. Private Wiggins was killed in Perryville, Kentucky on October 8, 1862.

Benjamin Abbot Traywick, Ben's paternal great-grandfather, was a First Sergeant in the Confederate Army, Company G, 28th Infantry (2nd Mountain Regiment Tennessee Volunteers). Sergeant Traywick participated in all of the battles waged across Tennessee and Mississippi, from Chattanooga to Shiloh. At the end of the war, he resumed farming on acreage owned by the family.

Like his predecessors, Ben T. Traywick was military minded and enlisted in the U.S. Navy during World War II although he was only 15 years old, being tall for his age. Assigned to the U.S.S. Jenkins DD447 (Fletcher Class Torpedo Destroyer), attached to the amphibious forces in the Pacific, he had earned ten Battle Stars and a Presidential Citation by his eighteenth birthday. He served a second hitch in the Navy in the late 1940s, most of it in China. When the Communists overran China, he was on the last ship to evacuate Tsingtao. The remainder of his enlistment was spent on the battleship Missouri.

Ben graduated from Tennessee Technological University with a B.S. Degree in Chemistry in 1953. After spending thirty years in exotic and high explosives in such places as Oak Ridge (Atomic); Sacramento (Missiles); and southeast Arizona (mining); he retired at the age of fifty-six.

Now he spends his time writing, researching Tombstone history, and visiting the far places in the American West and Mexico.

His first article was about a hillbilly sailor, called Saltwater McCoy. It was sold to "Our Navy" Magazine in 1957 and turned into a series. Ben has been frequently published in the Tombstone Epitaph since 1963. Since that beginning long ago, he has written more than six hundred newspaper and magazine articles. In addition, he has written forty-one pamphlets and books. His collection of "Earpiana" and Tombstone material is one of the best in existence anywhere.

Having been duly appointed by the Mayor and the City Council, Author Traywick is Tombstone's first and only City Historian to date. Ben and his wife, Red Marie, have lived in Tombstone since 1968. They have three children, Virginia Lynn, Mary Kate and William Maurice plus three Grandchildren; Benton Ivan, Rachel

Red Marie and Ben Traywick

Marie and Joshua Cody. They are co-founders of the "Wild Bunch" and "Hell's Belles," now famous after twenty-two years in the O.K. Corral and one hundred sixteen films as of 1993.

Together, Ben and Marie have created the Tombstone Book Series, a number of volumes that depict the local history as it actually was. It is their wish that you will find these volumes both interesting, entertaining and enlightening even as they have experienced in writing them.

Notes

Notes